When I Was a Child

Exposing and Overcoming Childhood Trauma

Visionary Author
Mia C. Turner-Whitley

©Copyright 2021 Mia Turner-Whitley

All rights reserved. This book is protected under the copyright laws of the United States of America.

ISBN: 978-1-954609-08-2

No portion of this book may be reproduced, distributed, or transmitted in any form, including photocopying, recording, or other electronic or mechanical methods, without the written permission of the publisher, except in the case of brief quotations embodied in reviews and certain other non-commercial uses permitted by copyright law. Permission granted on request.

For information regarding special discounts for bulk purchases, please contact LaBoo Publishing Enterprise at staff@laboopublishing.com.

All information is solely considered as the point of view of the authors.

The Holy Bible, King James Version. Cambridge Edition: 1769; King James Bible Online, 2019. www.kingjamesbibleonline.org

Scripture quotations marked (NIV) are taken from the Holy Bible, New International Version®, NIV®. Copyright © 1973, 1978, 1984, 2011 by Biblica, Inc.™ Used by permission of Zondervan. All rights reserved worldwide. www.zondervan.com

Scripture quotations marked ESV are from the Holy Bible, English Standard Version, copyright © 2001 by Crossway Bibles, a publishing ministry of Good News Publishers. Used by permission. All rights reserved.

Table of Contents

Introduction 1

The Ugly One – Felecia Hudson 5

A Drunk Can't Raise No Kids – Andrea Riley 17

He Loves Me; He Loves Me Not He Loves Me
(Maybe) – Perita Adams 27

The Abused Child – Liz Turner 41

Identity Found – Kayla Roberts 53

Trauma for Me as a Child – Shirley Lancaster 63

From Trauma to Testimony – Lakisha L. Tucker 79

Not a Daddy's Girl – Charlene Atchison 93

A Passion to Forgive – Cammie Stateman-Pitts 99

The Mirror – Belinda Strother 111

About The Visionary Author 121

Introduction

Childhood trauma is one of the saddest of all the traumatic experiences one can face. During childhood, life should be less stressful and contain wonderful memories of fun, laughter and growing pains. For many, this is not the case. For them it was about the harsh words, terrible beatings, and sexual molestation from a loved one! For these dear children, their innocence was taken away from them, never to return. These children had their childhood stolen and were placed in an adult situation with an immature frame of mind. For some, this world was so common they thought abuse was a natural part of life. They protected their abuser and built unhealthy relationships because the adult had manipulated the mind of the child.

Childhood trauma that is untreated can spill over into adulthood manifesting itself through unhealthy relationships, and or health issues, as the person continually asks "why me?" Many of these adults relive the trauma over and over by hitting replay. The personal torture can be unbearable and unforgivable. At some point, unless there is a rewriting of their narrative, they become a prisoner of their past.

The authors of *When I Was A Child - Exposing and Overcoming Childhood Trauma* will take us on a private tour of their traumatic experiences. We will read the pain and then the point where their mindsets and life changed for the better!

After reading perhaps you will walk away with a plan on how to escape the prison of your past, rewrite the narrative, and triumph over trauma!

When I Was a Child

Felecia Hudson currently resides in San Antonio, Texas where she is a Nurse Educator. She is the Director and Founder of The FAB Life, an organization that helps women to believe in themselves and go after their dreams. She believes that everyone has been created with a divine calling, and like a puzzle piece, we all fit in some way or another into the bigger plan of God.

She desires to inspire and empower women to believe this about themselves and to begin their personal journey of putting their imprint on the world.

Felecia enjoys taking vacations and reading books that inspire her and help to improve her mindset. Felecia considers her faith and her family to be most important to her.

The Ugly One

Felecia Hudson

"Sticks and stones may break my bones, but words will never hurt me," has to be the biggest lie ever told to mankind.

I remember that night so vividly. I felt like I was outside of myself. I was tired of my life; I was tired of my heart aching. I . . . was . . . tired . . . I thought, "That's it, I don't want to do this anymore." I was ready to kill myself. At 25 years old, I was ready to end it all. I'd suffered from depression for as long as I could remember, though I was never clinically diagnosed. It wasn't just sadness I experienced, it was heavy, dreadful darkness—I was aching, and it hurt physically. I had no energy and chose to be in the dark all the time. I didn't even open the blinds in my house. I'd come home from work and get in bed. I weighed almost nothing because I didn't eat. Strangely enough, I found comfort in all that sadness and darkness. I needed help, but I thought only people with "real problems" sought help from mental health specialists. Seeking help for something like anxiety and depression seemed like it was so taboo back then. No one sought help, you just dealt with it. Well, I was at my breaking point. I couldn't take any of the aching, the hurting, the crying, the sadness, and the anxiety anymore. I just wanted it to end because it hurt so badly.

My identity was stolen from me when I was just a little girl, but not through sexual molestation or any type of physical abuse. It was stolen by someone who spoke three simple words into my life. When you think about childhood trauma, you don't think about the power of words and the trauma they can bring. From the moment the words were spoken, I spent years trying to find the identity that was taken away. The funny thing is, I didn't know it was lost, and I surely didn't know how to find it. Where would I even look?

I was a teeny tiny little girl of about eight years old, from New Castle, Pennsylvania. It is a small town nestled between Ohio and Pittsburgh, where pretty much everybody knows everybody. I grew up in the 1980s; the best era in my opinion. I loved music by Whitney Houston and Janet Jackson, and Michael Jackson just topped it all off. Hip hop and rap were hitting the scene. I'd probably go back to that era if I could. I wasn't what one would consider cute in the 80s. I was darker skinned, very skinny, frail, and my body hadn't quite caught up to my head. One day, I was outside playing with my younger sister and there was a group of teenagers standing by, hanging out. I don't know if I was trying to hear their conversation, or the words were just spoken so loudly and carelessly they traveled easily to my ears. I have two sisters, one older and one younger. It sounded like two of the teenagers were making a comparison of the three of us and one male teenager said to another, ". . . no, the ugly one, right there." That conversation caught my attention and just as I looked at them, he pointed at me. The moment those words were spoken, even by someone so insignificant in my life, crushed my world. It was like a clam shell had closed around me and trapped me inside. I would remain enclosed in that shell for the greater part of my life.

My nickname when I was little was Kojak. Yep! As in Telly Savalas, Kojak. He was a detective in a drama series and was known for his bald head. According to my family, I didn't have a stitch of hair on my head until I was two years old. My uncle thought it was cute to call me Kojak. Innocent, right? I experienced the worst embarrassment and anxiety being called that name in the presence of my friends or anyone else, especially a boy! So, imagine, by the time I was a teenager, I had no self-esteem and many other issues from being labeled "the ugly one," and because my entire family called me Kojak. I lived in a strange place in my mind as a little girl and no one understood that.

Having a big head and having the nickname from hell made me famous amongst my peers. So, first let me say, hide and seek had to be the best neighborhood game we all played, especially when it was just about to get dark outside. When I was about 11 years old, I can recall there was a hide and seek chant made up about me. This is where the famous part comes in. The seeker would close their eyes and yell "Forehead!", while the hiders would yell, "Kojak!" This was by far one of the most humiliating things that has ever happened to me. I played along with the other kids as if it didn't bother me, but I had such a sad, broken heart when I heard those words. "Why couldn't I just be one of the cute girls?" I'd ask myself.

Who would think a few little words could hurt someone? It's all in fun, it's just innocent little chatter, right? I'm certain the teenager didn't think his words would cut me to the core like they did. I'm certain the kids playing hide and seek thought nothing of that hide and seek chant. I am certain the bully at school thought nothing of her bullying, but their words and their actions were deadly. The little girl died the day she was called the ugly one, and well into adulthood I thought my life would never be okay.

Throughout the years, when something negative would happen, it would somehow lead me back to that same broken little girl. If I failed at something, the hurt little girl rose up. If I had a breakup or experienced something unpleasant in a relationship, the rejected little girl rose up. Every single time something didn't go the way I planned, I blamed it on the ugly little girl. Of course, a root of my pain was rejection, and I developed self-destructive behaviors out of that root that brought on more rejection. It was like I would subconsciously place myself in positions to be rejected. When you truly don't care about yourself, you will allow any and every one to have their way with you. I thought that if I gave myself away to someone physically, all my hurt and pain would go away because my beauty would then be affirmed. But it was like building a house—starting with the foundation—adding brick on top of brick until I eventually ended up with a complete structure. It's been hard to tear that house down, especially when you don't know it's there and you think your behavior is normal. I am still tearing that foundation down, piece by piece. I learned early on that if I started turning the rejection onto people, they couldn't hurt me first. I realized later though that most people were not rejecting me and the rejection I felt really was self-imposed. I just believed everyone would reject me because I saw myself as the ugly one. I thought it was the ugly people that got rejected, right? My thinking was so twisted.

The anxiety I had was completely overbearing. I was easily embarrassed and everything made me uncomfortable. I didn't feel comfortable being around a lot of people. My ugliness just stood out. The shell I'd crawled into at eight years old was still enclosed around me. I never wanted to stand out. God forbid a teacher would call on me in the classroom, as surely it would draw attention to my ugliness. On top of that I felt everyone was watching me! I couldn't breathe, my heart was racing, and it was so overwhelmingly uncomfortable; all this because I was labeled the ugly one.

Words are powerful beyond measure. Proverbs 18:21, KJV, says, "Death and life are in the power of the tongue" and this I know to be so true. Words can either bring life and lift someone up, or they bring death and can destroy a person. "The ugly one," are words that are seemingly insignificant, but they killed a little girl's soul that day. I know it wasn't the young man's intention to hurt me. In fact, he probably had no clue that I heard him. But "the enemy comes only to steal, to kill and to destroy" (John 10:10 NIV), and that was the enemy's intention that day. For twenty-plus years "the ugly one" did just that—those words stole my innocence and purity, they killed my soul and sent me down a path of self-destruction.

Satan knew from the beginning the power that lay within that little girl. He knew she was carrying a purpose and a destiny that would impact so many people. The little girl did not know this purpose and calling was within her. We were created with a predetermined destiny according to Ephesians 2:10, NIV, "We are God's masterpiece created in Christ Jesus to do good works which God prepared in advance for us to do." Jeremiah 1:5, NIV says, "Before I formed you, I knew you, before you were born, I set you apart; I appointed you as a prophet to the nations." Before time, God knew me and when He created me, He had a purpose that only He and I would truly realize. I believe we come into the world knowing fully what we are to do here, but before we can understand the purpose that lies within, the enemy tries to snatch it away.

We are responsible for our words. The woman I am today knows how important the delivery of words is, because it was words that tried to take her out. I have made it a habit to tell every little girl I encounter how beautiful she is no matter her color, ethnicity, nationality, or hair texture; all little girls were fearfully and wonderfully made in the image of our creator God. They all need to hear it; I needed to hear it, and I longed to hear how beautiful I was! Because of this longing, I did what I thought was best to do in order to feel beautiful and accepted. I was a people pleaser even to the point of doing things I didn't feel comfortable doing to please others, mostly men. I allowed myself to be used by countless men, thinking it would make me feel better about myself and more beautiful. Actually, something died in me every single time I did anything I wasn't comfortable with. I just wanted to feel beautiful. I longed to feel beautiful.

In 2006, I was stationed in San Antonio, Texas, at Fort Sam, Houston. When I first got the orders that I would be going, I didn't feel good—I did not want to go to Texas. All I could think of was horses and cowboys, and neither were of any interest to me. I'm a girl from the northeast, so where would I fit in in Texas? Little did I know that San Antonio, Texas, would be where my life would change forever. Shortly after I moved here, I joined a local church and really started to learn and grow into the image that God created me in. I started learning about God, not from a legalistic standpoint of do's and don'ts, but from a relationship filled with the authentic love of the Father. Romans 8:28, KJV says, "And we know that all things work together for good to them that love God, to them who are the called according to His purpose." This scripture became very real in my life when I entered the next season of my life.

In 2008, I went on a mission trip to South Africa with some women from my church. Our purpose for going was to empower young women, and to help them understand who they are. Prior to leaving, each of us was given a topic to prepare to speak about with the girls. Are you ready for this? My topic was "How you see yourself." I was confused at first because I didn't know seeing yourself in a certain way was a thing. I didn't think I saw myself in any kind of way, so how could I tell these teenagers they should see themselves the way God sees them? I had a ton of anxiety leading up to this trip because I just didn't get it—how were we supposed to see ourselves? First, I felt like nobody to be speaking into someone else's life. "They will see right through me," I told myself. "I don't really think anything of myself and I know they will see this when I open my mouth to speak." Amid thinking all these things, I studied the Bible in regard to the topic I had to present to these young girls. The Bible showed me like a mirror who I was and who I was created to be. I was amazed at what it said about me and what God showed me through the written word.

I didn't believe it was possible for me to hear from God back then; that was for the pastors and the preachers, the teachers and the evangelists, but not me. I know now He was talking to me throughout that entire season. Through the process, He was healing me and restoring me with the very words He would have me speak to the girls. God gave me the idea to use mirrors to illustrate some points to the girls. I didn't know how this would work, but I did a segment where I gave every girl a mirror and had her look into it. Next, they were to tell me what image they saw of themselves. One girl said, "I see pimples!" and we all laughed. Another said, "I see someone I don't like." As it got deeper, some girls didn't want to look in the mirror, they wouldn't even pick up the mirror off the table. That moment revealed to me that so many young girls, like myself, are struggling with their self-image, and I had to do something about it. If they're struggling with what they see and feel on the outside, then they most certainly are struggling with their self-worth. Who knows what was destroyed in them, or what words were spoken over them? Who knows what was done to them to give them such an altered self-concept? That trip and that exercise had such a profound impact on me and I know God had it in His plan. I really saw how altered my image was of myself, but better yet, God showed me how to see myself the way He sees me.

During this season, God brought "the ugly one" incident back into my mind. He didn't do it to hurt me. He did it so He could heal me and use me. He showed me that no matter how broken my situation was, He could use it to heal others. I believe it was during my studies that God reminded me of how those words had affected me and the path of self-destruction that I went on from there on out.

Since I have accepted Jesus Christ as my Lord and Savior, my life has completely changed. I no longer see myself as "the ugly one," but as my Father sees me. Amazing things happen when you see yourself from the perspective of your true creation—my entire outlook changed. While I am becoming who God created me to be, my life is ever evolving. My self-worth, self-image, and self-concept are so different. I know who I am, and no one can tell me differently. I know what I was created to do, and I am confident God has even more He will reveal to me. The damaged little girl tries to rear her head sometimes, and that's okay. It is a subtle reminder I am still on this journey and my Father is with me. It's exciting to know I have a very important assignment here on earth. I have a very important purpose and a very important calling to make sure people hear the message. What the enemy meant for harm and evil, "God intended it for good to accomplish what is now being done, the saving of many lives" (Genesis 50:20)!

Even as an adult, words still affect me to the core. Recently, someone shared with me what they thought about the assignment God had given me to impart to women. It went against what I knew in my heart that God had purposed me to do. Their words made me question everything He had done up to this point in my life. I really thought they knew more than I did about the purpose God placed inside me. I thought God had either taken back what he called me to do because I'd messed up somewhere along the way, or that I had completely made this calling up in my head. How could I feel so strongly about something I know God told me to do and then, in an instant, find out I was wrong? Because of someone's words? I have discovered the enemy will try to use words to destroy me. The enemy is still using words to get me off track from what I know I was called and purposed to do. Proverbs 12:18 says, "the words of the reckless pierce like swords, but the tongue of the wise brings healing."

I leave you with this: WORDS ARE POWERFUL. They can build up and edify, or they can tear down and destroy. Words can completely damage a person's self-esteem, or they can build one's self-esteem. Don't be a dream killer. Don't be a destiny killer. Make it a habit to uplift and encourage. Your intention may not be to hurt that person, but ask yourself, "If someone said this to me or about me, how would it make me feel?" If it doesn't make you feel loved, then don't say it. Our words should make people feel loved even after they've left our presence.

This is my journey from ashes to beauty, and even in the beauty there remains a journey. Yet, I am ". . . confident of this, that he who began a good work in [me] will carry it on to completion until the day of Christ Jesus." ~ Philippians 1:6, NIV

 Ms. Andrea Riley is a single mother of three, Professional, Veteran member of the MS Air National Guard and a Best-Selling Author. Her journey is centered on raising awareness regarding Mental Health and Recovery. Ms. Riley is Mental Health First Aid Certified. She serves as a Statewide Autism Initiative Trainer. Ms. Riley is a 2018 graduate of the State Executive Development Institute at the Stennis Institute of MSU.

Ms. Riley serves as the Client Services Deputy Director for South MS Regional Center in Long Beach, MS, overseeing coordination of services for the people served in their Community Residential and Day Service programs.

Ms. Riley holds a Bachelor's Degree in Public Health, a Master's Degree in Public Administration and a Doctoral level Education Specialist degree in Adult Education.

Ms. Riley's written works include the chapter entitled "Mommy is Depressed" in the collaborative Best Seller, "The Mom in Me" and her testimonial work Valley to Victory.

A Drunk Can't Raise No Kids

Andrea Riley

You know how people say that people are a product of their environment anytime they do something and come from a background that is not so good. Have you ever stopped to think we never hear that when someone does something awesome? The association of negative actions with environmental factors far outweighs the association of good actions with environmental factors. While often the negative actions are a result of how a person was raised, sometimes the positive actions are also a result of how a person was raised despite their environment. Some people use a negative background to push them to do better, while others sink into a vicious cycle. Even though our parents drank, none of the four of us are alcoholics. Until about three years ago, none of us really drank at all unless it was a birthday or something.

Often in our life, we do not realize how trauma from our childhood shapes the way we see certain areas of our lives. We think it is just something we like or dislike. Sometimes, it is because of something we went through during childhood. When I spoke with my mom about my childhood trauma, I thought she would say "no do not write on that." I was shocked and grateful when she said, "I am not ashamed and make sure you tell it all, tell how I almost died from alcohol poisoning and how a drunk can't raise kids, so I quit drinking so I could raise my own kids." Growing up after my mother stopped drinking, I never stopped to think about the journey to sobriety because she just stopped drinking, and it was simple. I would see the sadness in my mom's face when she would look at some of my female family members, seeing who she used to be as she told them her famous line "a drunk can't raise no kids; I tried it, and it don't work." When I was in eighth grade, I accidentally left a suicide letter on my mom and dad's table by the bed and of course my mom found it. Can you believe SHE PUT ME OUT? Yes, put me out, honey. It was her own childhood trauma, her own self-medicating, and years of trying to rebuild her sobriety and be a good mother that drove her to this extreme. They literally lived about three miles from one another anyway, so for me it was a win-win in my mind as I could go home when I wanted.

I remember clearly, she sent me over to my biological paternal grandparents, however, it took me years to realize her putting me out had nothing to do with me. One thing she said to me as I packed my things is, "Suicide is one of the most selfish things you could ever do." However, I didn't care, as I thought it was selfish of her to drink like she did. I thought it was selfish of her to crawl into a bottle and we had to empty a garbage can full of vomit!

Now, in her defense, my grandparents kind of spoiled me, so I preferred to stay with them anyway because I could get my way.

It wasn't until years later, as we casually had a conversation about God and life, I learned at that point in my mom's life she was walking into her own sobriety and healing in places she'd been wounded, so in reality she didn't have the tools to deal with what I was dealing with in that moment. My mom would write in those black and white composition books back then. It was sort of like her diary and I was nosey, I read them. She would leave them in the bathroom, probably where she did most of her writing. Looking back, I can see my mother was depressed. She also had many struggles with depression and trauma, and that is why she can so easily relate to me. Yet, back then, she was unable (not unwilling), to help me because she too was in that place. However, my mom and dad were very open with us about life issues and things such as education, sex, decisions and things of that nature. Now, drinking was not necessarily something discussed. At that time in African American culture, depression and really dealing with mental health issues were somewhat taboo. So, in her having to learn how to deal with her own childhood trauma, heal, forgive, and move forward in life, to be a good parent was difficult. My mother and father were both drinkers, however, their attitude when they drank was the polar opposite to their personalities. My mom was a humbuggish drunk. Now, she never did anything to us, but Lord, she and Daddy fought like cats and dogs when she was drunk. Dishes? Oh Chile, they were broken from being thrown at Daddy. Daddy was a get-drunk-and-go-to-bed person, and he didn't even care if he had friends over. They all knew him so well that once he was into a bottle, they expected he would leave them and go to bed, period. So, when Daddy drank, it didn't bother me because I knew he would not cause any ruckus. But, now, I am not excusing the fact he drank too much.

My siblings and I often laugh about the many fights between our parents when we would have to run down the street to get another family member, usually our grandmother, my cousin Tina or Theresa, to come and do something. Even though we laugh about it now and even my parents laugh about it and talk about how crazy they were, my mom will often say, "Thank God I don't drink anymore." Honestly, I thank God for her because those were hard days for me emotionally.

Mama was a drink-until-you-pass-out person. You had to put her in a tub, clothes and all, to wake her up. The last time, her 32nd birthday, she almost died from alcohol poisoning. Oh, we watched them party and drink all night! Even as children, when we were told to stay in the room, we were peeking, laughing at them, and even entertaining them as they partied and drank. Then, we saw the after-effects: Mama in bed for days throwing up, unable to do anything. I remember being so mad when she was like that. Like what is so great about going through this if this is what it takes to have a good time? I recall I was about 10 years old and feeling so angry that she cared more about parties and drinking than me.

She and my cousins often went out to clubs and whoever was available would keep us. At that time, there was a family friend who volunteered to keep us and did unspeakable acts to us. I was furious, and a sense of hatred built in me each day about this. I couldn't understand why they kept leaving us with him. I didn't realize they didn't know what was happening; I was a child, and all I knew was the person I felt should have been protecting me was out drinking and partying while this man had his way with us. He even lived in the house with us and would do things to me. Then one night, my dad got up and I am pretty sure he saw me scurry back to my room as this man had told me to once he knew my dad was up. My dad was a quiet spirit when something bothered him. All I know is the next day, the man was gone and I have never seen him again.

Now at this point, the family friend/cousin was the second one to molest me and I was truly just full of hatred. I listened to my mom and dad talk about a Christmas when they got us bikes and I "refused to ride" the bike. Now in reality, even as a child, I thought, "Do they really not know or remember why I couldn't ride the bike?" They often told the story of how I refused to walk and I remember my uncle carrying me on his back to and from the restroom and stuff however, the reason I couldn't walk was because my older cousins had crawled through the window of our home where me and my sister was sleeping and took me into our bathroom and raped me, I probably was about six or seven at that time. I remember it like it was yesterday. Many times, with trauma, you suppress it or you remember it. For some reason, I have always remembered it all. I never could understand why they acted like I was just faking and didn't want to ride the bike, when in my mind, I really thought they all knew I was raped. As I got older, I settled in my spirit that maybe they didn't know or maybe they didn't want me to know that they knew and felt talking about it would re-traumatize me. Either way, as a child, I was pissed off.

I was like, "How can they act like this man didn't do what he did to me?" I said nothing for years, I just laughed it off and went on until one day, about two years ago, my mom and aunts (cousins) came down for my aunt's birthday. In the country, all the older cousins are referred to as aunts and uncles. We were headed to get some things for a paint and sip we were going to for her birthday and I EXPLODED, I blurted out everything that had happened. It was like something took over me and I had to get it out! I couldn't hold it in any longer. At that time, I still did not have the courage to talk to my parents about it, but I knew my aunts would.

I didn't know how to process all the emotions I felt; I was just angry. I was angrier because I felt no one cared. No one ever thought enough to ask me why my attitude was so bad or why I was so hateful. I was angry I didn't know how to process my emotions and I hated my mother for the image in my head of her drowning in alcohol, unable to wake up. I hated her for having to bring the trash cans to the side of the bed as she hung over them and threw up all the whiskey she drank the night before. I hated her for making me feel like I was unwanted, and I would end up like that. But she put the bottle down and decided she needed to raise her children instead of drinking her pain away when I was around 10 years old.

The other side of this was the damage was already done. Chile, I grew up reckless and promiscuous, and I was probably the most toxic person in relationships back then. I did care, but I was so used to emotional abandonment, that I often made sure I wasn't caught slipping. I did everything I could to avoid being vulnerable.

You better believe that before you do anything like cheating to hurt me, I've already got one up on you and I'll file it away, so when you hurt me, I can trump you. Just toxic! However, once I had kids of my own, I became determined none of this would happen to them. I stopped partying, drinking, going out, and I am not a fan of my daughter staying with anyone, regardless if they are family or not. I was also determined to heal from my experiences. In reality, I wasn't hateful or mean. I wasn't this horrible person I had become drowning in pain, anger, and misery. It was during a time when I was focusing on healing that I saw how the drinking and fighting really affected me to the point where I can't stand to be around people who are drunk. I dislike arguing, fighting, and yelling. One time, when talking to my therapist about the fighting, it immediately made me anxious. My heart beat faster and I was agitated to the point I wanted to stop the session.

On the other side of that, our parents showed us what it meant to stand with one another through the roughest of times. They rooted us in God and education, making sure that regardless of what they did, they wanted better for us. My mom often said, "Do what I say, not what you see me do." In retrospect, and even now, that was the craziest thing in the world to me. However, it helped me because I didn't want to be what she was when she was drinking. Watching my mother's faith and love for God grow after sobriety was a defining moment as we grew up. She didn't go to church every Sunday, but she studied her Bible daily. She taught us various things from the Bible and always told us to never compromise the Word of God and let no man deter us from what God says in His Word.

In conversations with my mom about her past, sobriety, and walk with Christ, she has helped me understand how to work through and forgive as she too has had to because the same thing happened to her as a child. I didn't even know that until this past year. It was like a light bulb moment as I realized the self-medicating with alcohol and drugs for her was tied to her own childhood trauma. Thus I began the journey to break the cycle for us. I had self-medicated when I was in my teenage and early adulthood years. I stopped back then and have picked none of it back up because I feel it is important for us to heal and forgive, as Christ has forgiven us. Childhood trauma turns into adult trauma if it festers! It is important as parents for us to remember when something happens in life that is traumatic for us, it is also traumatic for our children. Often, they do not understand how to process the emotions associated with the trauma. It is up to us as parents to help them through those issues.

Breaking the cycle, sets the course for us to be able to pour into others who have gone through this type of childhood trauma. It enables us to know that through Christ, we can be healed. We should be honest with our children about the trauma we have faced so they understand that while I am an adult, I understand the emotions they feel. We can understand the attacks on their mind because we too have been there. One day, my mom told me, "I never recognized the way you acted was depression and I really should have gotten you some help back then." Trauma and the reaction to it is different for everyone. Not everyone who is traumatized, depressed, or in crisis will display the same attitude and behaviors.

The wonderful thing about healing and forgiving is no longer having to carry the anger, misery, and unforgiveness around and pass it on to the next generation. Deciding to deal with my mental health, even if it meant going to therapy, and working through the hard process of healing, it was worth it. I had to forgive people, even if they did not deserve my forgiveness. I learned to walk in the deliverance of Christ.

The moment I stopped focusing on what they did and focused on my choice to live free of the traumatic grip of how it affected me, my whole outlook changed. I focused on this verse, "'For I know the plans I have for you,' declares the LORD, 'plans to prosper you and not to harm you, plans to give you hope and a future.'" Jeremiah 29:11, NIV. In grasping the concept that there was nothing that happened to me that was not already known, I realized God still chose me and kept me through it all. This change enabled me as a mother to discuss trauma and its effects with my own children, which in turn has enabled them to express their emotions so I can help them.

Childhood trauma often follows us into adulthood, we find ourselves dealing with the raggedy remains of its bitter grip. Flipping the trauma to triumph is the goal. The trauma and its ugly fragments are not meant to be carried for a lifetime.

Remember, the trauma was then, but the triumph is now. Is it an easy road to healing? NO! Healing from the trauma is triumph—forgiving is triumph. Refusing to remain in traumatic experiences is TRIUMPH. In the end, the goal is to triumph over the trauma to help others see that triumph is possible.

Perita H. Adams is a Certified Christian Life & Business Coach. She holds an Associate Degree in International Business and a Bachelor Degree in Organizational Communication. After studying abroad and missionary work in Africa, Brazil, Canada, China, Ecuador and many other countries she recognized her calling to inspire, educate, and motivate women to tap into their God-given gifts and talents to fulfill God's plan and purpose in their lives.

Perita is the owner of "GeneSIS Beginning Coaching & Consulting LLC." She has held many women's conferences and is a three-time bestselling author. Recently she has created a powerful 4-week course entitled "Birds of a Feather" created on the essence of "taking flight" in your life and letting strongholds go. This program was so well received she is currently working on Part 2.

Perita is a native of North Carolina. In her down-time she enjoys, reading, writing, art and spending time with her family.

HE LOVES ME; HE LOVES ME NOT HE LOVES ME (MAYBE)

Perita Adams

What is the definition of love? 1 Corinthians 13:4-8, NIV says, "Love is patient, love is kind. It does not envy, it does not boast, it is not proud. It does not dishonor others, it is not self-seeking, it is not easily angered, it keeps no record of wrongs." So if these things are true, why do so many people get it wrong?

I was only five when my mother married a man approximately 15 years her senior. He was a kind, teddy bear type with a big belly and a big heart. She was only 21 when she said, "I do." There was a car, a house, and the freedom that she longed for to start her life; however, little did she know her freedom wouldn't last for long.

My mother was one of 13 children and she grew up with a well-to-do parent. Her mother was the intelligent disciplinarian while her father was a sweet, humble man that everybody loved. She never needed or wanted for anything. So where did things go wrong with her selection of the nightmare she would endure? Did she not see the signs, or were they just too cleverly hidden?

Through a Child's Eyes

This story is very personal; however, I've wanted to share it for some time. I hope my childhood trauma saves the lives of other children. I was only two years old when they met, and things seemed to go well for quite some time. They had not yet married, but they did when their little boy (my half-brother) was three. We lived in a modest home, and my stepfather had a great job. Even as a young girl, I was glad such a kind man had taken on the duties of raising me and my sister as his own. It would be fair to say we appeared to be one big happy family.

Then Dr. Jekyll came into the picture. He looked like my new dad, but he was very mean to my mother. She was a young, beautiful lady with caramel features, long hair, and a bright smile. Even now, as an adult, it saddens me to tell you what happened next. Crash, bang, thump! I see my mother against the bedroom door being punched like a man! I'm literally in shock! I can't move! I'm frozen! The picture I have in my mind is as fresh as yesterday.

Stop the Violence

My reaction was to help my mom and not to hurt my stepfather, but to somehow "stop the violence!" I was helpless. I was five-years-old and screaming, crying, and asking God to save my mom. "Please, God,

Mom said you can do anything. I believe in you, so HELP!" Psalm 11:5, NIV says, "The LORD examines the righteous, but the wicked, those who love violence, he hates with a passion" and Colossians 3:19, NIV "Husbands, love your wives, and do not be harsh with them." As a babe in Christ, I was so confused about how such a loving God could allow this to happen? "STOP!" she cried to my step-father, "you're hurting me," as she tried to protect herself from a losing battle. I had a front-row seat that I didn't want for good versus evil. My sister was only a year older and came around the corner with a broom and mop that we used to help my mom get free. You may say that the broom and mop worked, or maybe it just got his attention, but I believe God heard my prayer. However, peace didn't last long.

God's Plan / Our Purpose

Jeremiah 29:11, NIV "'For I know the plans I have for you,' declares the Lord, 'Plans to prosper you and not to harm you, plans to give you hope and a future.'" For many years, I continued to see the abuse. My mother's self-esteem took a big hit. When she fought back, it would only agitate Dr. Jekyll even more. As I laid in my room at night, I kept wondering why it was happening. Would my mother survive this horrific abuse? What were his triggers, and how could she avoid them? I prayed, "God, you must have a plan to save my mom. Please, do it quick!"

There's a greater plan and purpose for you and your children. I often tell my life coaching clients, "If a situation is harming you and the joy you seek in your life, then that's not part of God's plan. Your destiny is greater than the danger you're in, so fight back."

Mama's Tears

"Mama, don't cry, God is on the way." I could see the fear and sadness in her eyes. My stepfather was a weekend alcoholic. So, like clockwork, he was sober by Sunday as if he had woken up from a trance. Monday through Friday, everything was mostly normal. As a child I hated the ABC store, which was the local liquor store in our community. Those very letters I saw every day in elementary school were different to what I witnessed happened when everybody crowded inside that store on the weekend. How could you sell something that brought harm to families like mine every weekend? Dr. Jekyll appeared every Friday and I would hear my mother cry as she tried to run away from her abuser. But one thing I knew for sure was that I was still praying.

You know the power of prayer is incredible. If you have ever heard a child pray, you know that's something innocent, sacred, pure, and purposeful. Psalm 30:5, KJV says, "Weeping may endure for a night, but joy cometh in the morning." I used to pray, "Mama, don't worry, joy is on the way!"

Grace + Mercy = Deliverance

For every bad day, the good ones outweighed them. Although my mother suffered abuse, ironically, her children were really never harmed physically. Yeah, we got the typical discipline as children to listen to your parents, behave in public etc. but thank God we experienced no direct harm, if you want to call it that. When my mom was happy, she was happy. Many times, she got out of harm's way by the grace of God. She would go over to her parents and spend the weekend there. The Bible was her closest confidant, outside of God himself. I could see the dim light in her growing brighter as she continued to go to church. That bright smile that she had started to appear. Her confidence, although still a little shaky, started to build. With freedom comes deliverance, and she started to take her life back and stand on her own feet.

I absolutely love that song by CeCe Winans, *Mercy Said No*. It just resonates about the true love God has for His children.

> The Mercy of God said…
>
> No, you can't have my daughter
>
> She's the daughter of a king and I don't just give her to anybody.
>
> No, you can't have her joy
>
> Because you didn't give it to her and you can't take it away
>
> No, you are not in charge. I Am!
>
> No, you can't have her life - Because I gave her life
>
> No, you can't have her hopes, her dreams - For I know the plans I have for her
>
> No, you can't have her power - Because greater is he who is here than he who is in this world
>
> No, simply because I Am the Lord God and I said so!

School Can't Teach Me This

I often went to school trying to concentrate and do my studies. School was where I escaped. I absolutely love to learn. Trivia is my best go to because I love expanding my knowledge of interesting facts. However, as a child, trying to balance the act of truly being a kid, but going home to a situation that was hectic was extremely difficult and sad. I often daydreamed in class about how to make the world a better place. Thus, now I'm a lifestyle coach (go figure). Remember, I said God has a plan and a purpose. The teachers were kind and taught me so much academically, but they couldn't fathom what I was going through on an emotional level. Often people stay in harmful relationships for their kids' sake, but often the children don't benefit. Believe me, I can tell you this from personal experience. When I went home, I would see my mom doing her best to get the house in order and prepare meals for the family before he got home. I would look at her and say to myself, "Doesn't she see what I see? The beauty, the brilliance, the 'I can do all things through Christ who strengthens me.'" Then I realized that my siblings and I were her strength. Therefore, I went to school and gave them my best, so she had something she could be proud of and hold her head up. Sometimes, I wanted to talk to the teachers about my situation merely to save my mother. But although I was just a kid, my mother, like most mothers in her predicament, had schooled us on the potential backlash that might occur. So I took it in stride and kept the family secret.

The world is changing ever so rapidly and I hope one day that children can ask for help at school without the additional consequences that may follow. To the mom battling a situation like this, you owe it not only to yourself but to your children to fight for a better life. In the meantime, teach your children how to pray because God is listening. Mark 10:13-16. NIV says, "People were bringing little children to Jesus for him to place his hands on them, but the disciples rebuked them. When Jesus saw this, he was indignant. He said to them, 'Let the little children come to me, and do not hinder them, for the kingdom of God belongs to such as these.'"

He Loves Me; He Loves Me Not; He Loves Me (I think)

As time went on, my mother got a job offer from Allstate, which was one of the top producing insurance companies at that time. I was super happy for her and now she saw herself as we did—smart, outgoing, and capable. Sure, it wasn't the FBI forensics job she had dreamed of, but her fate was changing for the better.

As you could imagine, my stepdad didn't want her to take the job, she had already accepted but then reluctantly declined. The fact that she actually considered it let me know there was hope for her. Seeing her in a new light, he began to change. He was more loving and drank less. I was now a teenager, and I thought, "Yes, God can change anybody." I was really happy because he was a sweet man with a big heart. I understood how demons could wreak havoc on a man's soul. My relationship with the Lord started as a very young girl, so my mom used to say. It wasn't that I only prayed for my mom, but I also prayed for my stepdad and that God would change his heart. At this point, I think it's important to stress that God could change my dad's heart, not my mother. Speaking from a woman's perspective, we often think we can fix people and that usually gets us into a lot of trouble. As things came to a dull roar, my mother finally took a job and her confidence went through the roof. Finally, our immediate family was thriving. I was predominately raised by my grandmother, who was strong, feisty, and smart, which made up for the controversy I endured at home. Nonetheless, I never wanted for anything except my mother's happiness. To be quite honest, I loved my stepfather and God rest his soul, I still do. No one knows but God, the demons of my stepfather's past. Time marches on and life is good. Then one day, just like a horror flick, Dr. Jekyll came back out. This time he was angry as ever. Why God?

Only this time my mother found the strength to leave. If you only knew my happiness and the sense of pride I felt for her courage. Mom was and still is my superwoman! Sometimes it just takes time to find yourself during a hardship in your life and she won. Nonetheless, her battle was not yet over. Ever wonder why they call it a testimony? It's because to learn the lesson of life, you will be tested, and my mother was no exemption to the rule. My stepdad wooed her back after a couple of years, and she went out of love and forgiveness. Ephesians 4:32, ESV says, "Be kind to one another, tenderhearted, forgiving one another, as God in Christ forgave you."

Again, everything was like *Leave It to Beaver* for those of you who remember the show. In essence, we enjoyed being a big happy family again. But as you might predict, it didn't last long. God has many gifts, but the strongest is LOVE and it can make you or break you. Life is full of testimonies, so it is never just one test. Sometimes you have to be retested until you pass. However, the idea is to learn the lesson so you can pass the test. Yes, my mother went back, but she remained a vigilant student of this part of her life and this time she aced her final exam. She left permanently.

The Hallelujah Moment

You know that moment when there is a divine shift and there's a major pivot in your life for the better? We all look for that glimpse of light at the end of the tunnel. My mom had finally found hers. John 8:12, NIV says, "When Jesus spoke again to the people, he said, 'I am the light of the world. Whoever follows me will never walk in darkness, but will have the light of life.'" For those who are still going through abusive relationships and your children see it, know that they are part of your strength and motivation to help you get through this. I only say your children are a part of your strength because you are still strong. Most people don't understand it and sometimes you may even feel alone in the process, but you're not because God is there.

Faith + Courage = Breakthrough

There were many nights as a child I cried for my mom. The mental trauma of watching someone you love in an earthly battle with spiritual undertones is unforgettable. Ephesians 6:12, KJV says, "For we wrestle not against flesh and blood, but against principalities, against powers, against the rulers of the darkness of this world, against spiritual wickedness in high places." My mother fought hard with prayer, persistence, hope, and faith, but her breakthrough came with courage. Most of the time I imagined being big enough, old enough, or strong enough to help her. But little did she know that as I watched her pray and talk to the Lord, she was teaching me how to pray. When things were out of order at home, she took us to church. There she found her peace. It was there she cried out for help and realized the battle wasn't hers. It was the Lord's. It was there she found her breakthrough.

The GeneSIS Beginning

John 1:1, NIV says, "In the beginning was the Word, and the Word was with God, and the Word was God." As I became a teenager and a young woman, I was very purposeful about not letting my history affect my destiny. According to the National Coalition Against Violence, a child who witnesses abuse is more likely to carry violence from one generation to the next, especially boys. I made up in my mind early on that I would not be a victim, nor an abuser. I stayed in the Word of God for guidance about what true love looked like. It became my mission to come alongside other women and make sure that no matter how hard life got, they recognized they were ENOUGH. The talent and gifts my mother possessed intellectually, spiritually, and mentally helped me to create my platform. By watching her endure her struggles and overcome them, it has blessed me to serve powerful women who once endured similar struggles, as a (Christian) Personal Life and Business Coach.

Genesis 1:1-5, ESV "In the beginning, God created the heavens and the earth. The earth was without form and void, and darkness was over the face of the deep. And the Spirit of God was hovering over the face of the water. And God said, 'Let there be light,' and there was light. And God saw that the light was good. And God separated the light from the darkness. God called the light Day, and the darkness he called Night. And there was evening and there was morning, the first day." I'm not sure who needs to hear this, but there is joy in the morning.

Christ over Covid-19

I can only imagine the endless cases of abuse that have occurred during this pandemic due to isolation. Believe me, there are so many children who have suffered in silence with no way out and that breaks my heart. My only hope is that they have a relationship with God and know that they are not alone. For the many women who have endured, and still endure domestic abuse, please reach out for help. Right now, it is important that friends and loved ones keep check on one another. I know pride is an issue, but you and your children deserve better. It may take some time to pick up all the pieces and you may have to crawl before you walk, but you will thrive again. John 16:33 says, "These things I have spoken unto you, that in me you might have peace. In the world you will have tribulation, but take heart, I have overcome the world."

He LOVES me; He LOVES me not. God LOVES YOU!

Resources:
National Domestic Violence Hotline:
1-800-799-SAFE (7233)

For personal coaching, speaking or media engagements contact:
Perita H. Adams-Certified Christian Life & Business Coach
The GeneSIS Beginning Coaching & Consulting LLC.
Website: www.thegenesisbeginning.com
Email: thegenesisbeginning@yahoo.com
IG: peritaadams

Author Jamie "Liz" Turner is a mother of two young kings, wife, and minister, who has built her platform of a healthy balanced life on the foundation of God's principles. God has blessed her to plant her feet in other countries as an International Prophetic dancer.

She has traveled across seas to deliver God's word and has become a mentor for many. Her educational background consists of a degree in the medical field along with a bachelor's in education. This chapter is just a glimpse of her life and how far her journey has led her, and there is more to come.

THE ABUSED CHILD

Liz Turner

One day, my mother dropped us off at big mama's house and left to go to work or school. My auntie asked if we wanted to play school, and my brother and I said yes because we knew we would get snacks. On this day, a female cousin came over to play with us as well, and we had a blast until it was time for a nap. My brother and I could not stand nap time, but I mean what kid really does. My auntie separated us into two different rooms, and she was in charge of watching over my brother during nap time and my cousin over me.

During nap time, I felt a warm pat on my back and realized it was my cousin patting me to sleep. I was not bothered by it because it seemed normal at first until the caressing began in other places. I was very scared and confused because this was an unfamiliar feeling. As a six-year-old little girl, there are things we are not supposed to be exposed to, but unfortunately, I was violated not only by a woman, but by someone who I believed to be family. Isn't family meant to protect you? I was terrified to the point that I did not tell anyone, not even my brother, who was my best friend. The next day, my mother asked me if everything was okay and I responded yes, but deep down I was crying and confused. This abuse continued for about a year and no one ever knew or was told.

My mother finally graduated from nursing school and my brother and I knew it was time to celebrate. My mother had promised us once she graduated college we would go to Disneyland, and we did. We had so much fun with it being just us and our mom, but we did miss our dad. One day, my mom brought a man home and introduced him to us as her boyfriend. We didn't know at the time what that meant. All we knew was that he started coming around a lot, being really nice, and cooking for us.

My brother and I had this little issue with wetting the bed, but to be honest, it was pure laziness. Our mom had warned us several times that we needed to get that under control because she was tired of washing sheets. Well, one morning I felt a sharp stinging pain hit the back of my legs and I screamed while leaping out of my bed. When I fully opened my eyes, it was my mom's boyfriend, and boy was I confused. My scream must have woken my brother because he was standing at attention right next to me. My mother was standing right next to her boyfriend and she could tell we were confused, so she ran to her room and grabbed a piece of paper. When she returned, she said this document right here says that he is your father now, and he has the right to discipline you. I was taken aback because not only had I just found out he was going to be my new dad, but he had permission from my mother to put his hands on me. However, I was a child and stayed in a child's place. After the chastising, our new dad told us to clean our rooms and take baths and never pee in the bed again, and sure enough, we never did. At the time, we did not know this form of abuse would be the new normal.

I was a little intimated by my stepfather because I had never had a man whoop me before, but it stopped me from being lazy. My stepfather taught me how to cook at the age of seven. He told me if I could learn how to boil water, I could cook anything, and he was right. The first thing I learned to cook was a boiled egg, and then malt-o-meal. He taught my brother and me to brush our teeth correctly, wash dishes, do laundry, and just be clean overall. His background was military, so trust me, a dirty house was out of the question.

One day my stepfather told us we were moving across the United States to Georgia. It happened so fast. Within a month, we were there. I hated that we had to move, so I stormed off and went into the room we would be staying in until we found a permanent place. Well, I guess the bedroom door slammed after I had stormed off in anger, because two seconds later my stepfather was yelling in my face asking why I had slammed the door, and that I did not pay bills, and then he slapped me upside my head. I was shocked that he was so mad because of a door, and my brother was too. We didn't tell our mom because we assumed he would tell her about the incident, but even if he didn't, I was already afraid of what he might do if he found out I told.

Two months later, we moved into our first apartment that we could call ours. It was a three-bedroom upstairs-downstairs, fully furnished apartment. When we moved in, I noticed that the neighborhood was full of kids and it had a basketball court with a park. It was amazing to have my own room again and be around kids our age. Everyone was happy and everything seemed to go well, even to the point my mom allowed my stepfather to get a dog. He got an all-white Pitbull with a black patch around his eye, and his name was DMX. I could not stand that dog because he would always use the bathroom in the house, and I would have to clean it up because I was the oldest. We stayed in those apartments for about two years and then moved to college park. The next few years we moved about three more times and I am still unclear why.

One day my mother asked my brother and I if we would like a brother or sister, and we lit up the entire room with joy. We were excited to have another play buddy. I was 10 at the time and my brother was nine. When our new baby brother came into the world, everything in my world changed.

My stepfather became even stricter after the new edition. I knew that once his son got here, even though he was my brother, he thought we would wreak havoc. I walked around the house for months on eggshells, making sure I didn't make my stepfather mad because I knew it was just a matter of time before I was punished for something my baby brother had done. But so much time passed by until I honestly thought nothing would happen to me. Until one day my stepfather came home and was yelling at the top of his lungs. I ran out of my room and he was fussing about a bleach stain in the middle of the living room floor. Of course, my brothers were clueless, and my stepfather looked dead at me to blame because I am the oldest. I pretty much knew what the drill was and was prepared to get a whipping, so I went to use the bathroom first. When I was coming out, my stepfather was standing at the door and he called over my brother and told him to check under the sink for the bleach. When he did, we all noticed the top was off, and our baby brother must have gotten into it by mistake. Well, at least that's what I was thinking and must have been wrong because within the next few seconds I realized this grown man's hands were around my throat and choking me.

The next thing I knew, I woke up from hitting my head on the ground because I had passed out and dropped to the floor. He and my brother were standing over me, calling my name as I slowly came to. My stepfather said he didn't realize he was choking me that hard, and he was sorry. Of course, I figured he told my mom because that's what married people do, right? More whippings came after he lost his job as if he was bored. For example, he was not fond of the dishwasher because he didn't believe it did a good job, but my mom would use it from time to time. Well, one day I was told to put the dishes up in the dishwasher and I did as I was told, but once again I did something wrong because the familiar sting of my stepfather's leather belt woke me later. He dragged me into the kitchen and pulled glass cups down, asking me why there were water spots on the glass. I explained to him it came from the dishwasher and he whipped me some more. After he was done, I was told to re-wash every dish in the kitchen and he didn't care that I had to get up for school in four hours.

After a few months of this and many more incidents, my willing love for him completely turned into loving him out of fear. Every time he walked through the door, my brother and I would run to give him hugs and kisses out of fear of being beaten later. We figured maybe if we showed him more love, he wouldn't be so mean. I would get whipped over everything that you could possibly think of just because I was the oldest. I then trained my brothers how to do things right because I was tired of getting in trouble because of them, let alone my own doings. The abuse stopped after one terrible incident with our baby brother.

My youngest brother was infamous for knowing how to throw a tantrum, and of course, he did as he was the baby. He got in trouble several times one day at daycare and his dad, my stepfather, went to pick him up from school, and then us afterward. When we got home, he said to our little brother he would get a spanking for acting out at school. So, he grabbed his little hand and dragged him to the back room, and spanked him. My brother must have fallen out during the spanking because we heard the hits and screams become louder! My other brother was so furious he grabbed his Louisville slugger and started walking toward our parent's bedroom door. I stopped him and talked some sense into him, saying it would be a suicide mission. About five minutes later, my stepfather appeared and went straight to the kitchen to grab a wooden spoon and then went back into the room. He beat my baby brother with a wooden spoon until it broke. My heart broke that day because he was helpless, and I could do nothing for him but hold him when his punishment was over. How could someone do that to a four-year-old child?

At that time, I could not understand why my mom was not around, and I did not know that she was working two jobs to keep a roof over our heads. Our stepfather worked on and off as an entrepreneur and a cable guy. Like always, we assumed he told my mom of the beating he gave our baby brother when my mom got home from work, but we were sadly mistaken. The next day, my brother and I caught the bus and went to school as normal. It was midday, and I was called to the principal's office to see my mother and my two brothers already there. My mom said we were being withdrawn from the school. I cried on the way to the car because I did not get to tell my friends goodbye. When we got in the car, my mom said she would explain everything when we got home. On the way home, we stopped by the store and bought our baby brother a set of blocks from his favorite toy store and we stopped for ice cream. I knew something was up because we only got ice cream when my mom or stepdad wanted to tell us something. When we got home, our stepfather was already there, which was a surprise to everyone because he was usually at work when we were at school. My mom told us to all go to our room, and we did.

The next thing we know there was a loud thud on the wall and then my parents' bedroom door slammed. I ran to see what had happened and to see if my mom was okay. She busted open the door, screaming and yelling at my stepfather. I really could not make out what was being said, but I knew it was serious. My mom grabbed me and said we were leaving. My brothers came around the corner and she instructed them to go back while she talked to me. I found out when my baby brother went to school that day, Child Protection Services (CPS) was called on my family.

Allegedly, when he went to the bathroom, he told the teacher it hurt to pull his pants down and he needed help. So, the teacher helped him and noticed bruises all over his back and buttocks. He immediately reported it to his supervisor and my mother was called along with CPS. My mom pleaded with them not to open a case and by the grace of God, they did not file. After she told me this, she said we were moving and for me and my brother to go pack our stuff. We did, and we left.

We ended up in Jonesboro, Georgia, in a two-bedroom apartment. I was 14 years old and very anxious to see what my new school would be like and the people. My first day was not bad. In fact, everyone welcomed me with open arms. I missed my old home and friends, but I knew my mom decided what we did, and we would have to follow. Three months passed, and I still hadn't seen my stepfather around and we had moved from the friend's house into an apartment with a creek behind it. I couldn't stand living by water because there were always rats or snakes in the back. One day I asked my mom where our stepfather was and she explained they were temporarily separated, and he might come back. I did not think twice about it after she said that because I was relieved. There would be no more unnecessary beatings or punishments or walking on eggshells to please him. Finally, I was at peace, or so I thought.

One day when I came home from school, my stepfather was in the living room. I was not surprised because I knew eventually, they would get back together. I just didn't know it would be that fast. I said hi and went straight to my room and started writing in my journal. About an hour later, my mother came into my room and asked me and my brothers to come into the living room. I realized my stepfather was gone, but I did not ask where he went because I honestly did not care as long as he was gone. My mother then asked my brother and me a question that would change the course of our lives. It was if we wanted to move to Texas, and we answered YES! The seven years of abuse were finally over!

After arriving in Texas, my mom suggested we should reach out to our real father and spend some time with him, and we did. I decided a few months later I wanted to live with my dad for half the school year, so I stayed. Two months later, I got a phone call from my brother who I missed very much. He said that our stepfather had moved to Texas and was living with them now. My blood rose because I felt like my mother had betrayed our family by going back to a man who did not value her. My brother begged me to come home, so I packed my things, and I left my dad's house.

My stepfather greeted me with a big hug when I came through the door, which is not something he would normally do. It did not phase me because I knew he would slip up and show his true colors again one of these days, and I prayed that at that time my mom would leave him for good.

One day our stepfather yelled for me and my brother to come up the stairs. We ran up the steps within seconds because we were all too familiar with that tone. My mother was upstairs too in their bedroom with our baby brother. We were standing in the family room and he asked us why there was a piece of paper on the floor. We both looked puzzled, so he said it had been there for three days and one of us should have picked it up by now. He was waiting to see if we would take the initiative to do so. My brother and I were so scared we still did not speak until he yelled, "Answer me." My step-sister came running out of our bedroom to see what was going on and stood next to me, looking just as puzzled. I said we had not seen it and we had just vacuumed as he asked us to do the day before. Then before I could even retract the next words that came out of my mouth, I asked, "Why didn't you pick it up, Dad, if you saw it first?" Then a burning sensation flew across my face and I flew into the wall and hit the floor. He had just slapped me!

My mother came running across the house to ask what had happened, as she'd heard a loud noise. She saw me holding my face and lying on the floor. She screamed at my stepfather at the top of her lungs, saying, "You never should hit a woman in the face; what is wrong with you?" They started arguing back and forth, and I realized this was Georgia all over again. Why God?

Wife/Mother/Grandmother/Minister/Author/Counselor/Motivational Speaker

Kayla R. Weatherall is a woman who does not look like what she has been through. Kayla is a co-author of "Phenomenal, That's Me! Still Standing." It's a book about how to overcome even when the situation looks like you will not survive.

Kayla overcame an 11-year physically abusive relationship to go into a 13-year verbal and emotional abusive relationship. Kayla has an AAS degree in Software Engineering, a minor in Professional Office Technology from Texas State Technical College. She also has a Bachelor of Theology from Word of Truth Bible College where she is now working on her Masters.

Kayla is a woman after God's own heart who was ordained and licensed in the ministry as a minister in 1998. God is always first in her life, followed by family and friends. God sent the love her life, Vincent, whom she has been married to for 5 years. Together they have 10 children and 19 grandchildren.

Kayla's passion is ministering to young women who are at risk of or struggling through teen pregnancies, domestic violence and self-esteem issues, her goal is to lead them out of those places as God lead her out. Through mentoring, teaching, and sharing, she encourages these women. She also assists with men by uplifting and encouraging them to be the Kings God called them to be.

weatheritallministry@gmail.com

IDENTITY FOUND

Kayla Roberts

The Bible teaches us, we move from glory to glory! What this means to me is our perfect God is always perfecting us, taking us from one level of glory to another. To get there, you go through a process. Trust me, I have been through the process. I have been refined! I understand going from glory to glory! Sometimes the process is not a pretty one, but a productive one.

If someone had told me when I was young that trouble was coming to my door and not only would it knock, but it would kick the door down and invade my life and shatter my world before I reached adulthood, I would not have believed them. I never imagined I'd have to face this kind of adversity. I never would have thought that I could go through what I have and make it out of it.

I learned at a young age what it was to have to struggle and go without. I grew up not having a lot, but we always made it work no matter what it was. I learned the value of a dollar at a very young age thanks to my grandparents, who started me working in the field at five years. God will prepare you for what you have to go through when you are young if you just receive it and obtain the lesson. Growing up with a single mother, my grandparents played a big part in my life. My father was killed while my mother was yet pregnant with me, so I never had the chance to meet him. Amid my loss, God gave me what I needed. God will always give you what you need, even when you don't know you need it. My mother later married the man that raised me as his own and will always be my father. He later taught me what real love was, even when I didn't want to learn the lesson or understand it.

I felt like an outsider when my mother had my younger sister because now all my siblings had the same father but me. When we took pictures, you could always tell I was different and the children and people around the neighborhood let me know. The children in the neighborhood teased me and picked on me, calling me names other than my own. As time went on, I learned to just stay in my shell and not talk. I started to be what other people wanted me to be, so they would let me play with them and be a part of their group. I never really ever knew my true identity, because it was easier, I thought, being someone else. As I got older, I changed even more to fit in. I sometimes hung out with the wrong type of people and faced things I knew were not right. This went on for years, and I was fine with it. When I was in middle school and high school, I was bullied because I did not have the name brand clothes they were wearing. Life was hard, and I thought about ending it many times, but I just could not go through with it.

Because of all the bullying and teasing, I had no self-esteem, and I almost felt no love. Not that my mother and father did not love me, I just knew I was different. At this point, I started doing things I should not have been doing. I was sneaking out and going to parties, talking to older guys, and drinking. They did not know me, and I was big for my age and I knew how to make myself fit in, for I had been doing this all my life. At some point, you know when to change your life, but I didn't, so I turned to men, drinking, and partying at a young age.

I became pregnant when I was 15 and embraced motherhood when I was 16 with nothing but a lot of confusion going on in my mind. The father was not in the picture, so I was a single mother in high school. After this, I turned to another man to lead me and help me. When this relationship started, I never thought I could love another. He helped with my child and treated her as if she was his own. He told everyone she was his, knowing that she wasn't. Sometimes, God will let you have what you want, even if it's not good for you. What started out good quickly went bad when I realized he had another girl he said was just a friend. I realized I didn't have to go through this, so I left him.

I was now a senior in high school and had moved on to someone else, but the young man stayed in my child's life and treated her as his own. Right before Christmas break, a young lady showed up at my locker. She approached me and began to accuse me of messing with her man because of his relationship with my daughter. I said nothing because I did not want any problems at school. He was at the locker with me, I told him that I could not talk to him and that I would walk myself to class. I wanted no problem with this young lady, so I tried to walk away. As I walked away, she pushed me. I snapped! There comes a point in your life when you just can't take anymore. I had been bullied and picked on all my life due to the lack of not having and wearing the things the other kids had. Like I said, we had little when I was growing up. At this point, I couldn't take anymore, and when she touched me, I pushed her head into the locker. Afterward, the principal asked me if was I okay and I started laughing. I said yes but they should check on her as she was the one bleeding. This was the beginning of a downhill spiral in my life.

I started back drinking and skipping school. Later, I found myself in a gang and getting into trouble that I really should not have gotten in to. I got back with my son's father and found myself pregnant with my second child while I was still in high school. After almost losing my child at three months, I had to have bed rest and could not continue with the rest of my class. Life really got rough for me at this time. I felt as if I were a failure and that I could not make it. Once my child was born, I went through postpartum depression. At this time, I tried to take my own life with a gun, but it jammed. God always has a plan for our life, even when we don't want to live. If God has a work for you, no matter what you go through, you will not leave this life until you complete it.

After my child was born and I got past all the postpartum, I started back doing what I was doing before by partying, clubbing, gang banging, and drinking. My son's father became verbally abusive, and I did not realize words could hurt that bad. I had heard that there was another young lady that had a baby with him just months before me, but I had no proof at the time. Then one day

I received a very disturbing phone call from a young lady saying that they had just had a baby together. I didn't know how to respond to that, so I just dropped the phone. My thoughts were expressed inward. I had two children and no job, and no place to go. After this happened, things got bad at home and my mother told me I had to leave her house because of what I was doing. She said, "Since you are doing grown folks things you need to act like you a grownup." I was only 18 and immature and I did not know how I could take care of myself and two small children.

I had no place to go, so I moved in with him to his mom's house. This was not the best choice, but at the time I thought it was. I felt it would keep me from being alone and keep us off the street with no shelter or food to eat. This went on for six months to a year, while he was still cheating. Being so young and not understanding what is means to really be loved, you can sometimes think love is one thing when it really is not. The fights started out with just words and later they got physical and got worse over the years. The one thing that never changed was that every fight ended with him saying I made him do it, and I believed him. I believed him because I still did not love myself and I did not have a self-identity at this point. With the same breath he would always say "I love you" and I was the best thing that had happened to him and he would never do it again. If I had a dollar for every time that I heard that I would have been rich. I thought that if I changed and did what he wanted me to do, he would not do it again. What I didn't understand is that it didn't matter how much I changed as I was only changing into who he wanted me to be—this change was not for me, but someone else. You can't change to stop abuse; you can only be delivered out of it. You can walk away, but until you change your own mindset and know who you are and fall in love with yourself, you will yet find yourself with an abusive partner. I tried to leave him and asked my mother if I could I move back home. I was 19 and pregnant with my third child. Once again, I was alone, with nowhere to go. I started living in run-down hotels when I could afford them with the government assistance. I fought for my respect from others, but did not respect myself. This went on for about two months until a friend found out and allowed me and my children to move in with her and her mother. I later got an apartment in a low-income apartment complex. My biggest mistake was allowing my son's father to move in. But I only felt love when he was around. At this point in my life, any love was better than no love at all. I fought there because I had not yet left the gang life. See, in the gang you feel you are a part of something. That something may not be what is best for you, but you have their back, and they have your back. I thought this was who I was, but I hated every day of my life at this moment.

I had my third child, and the relationship got worse, but God always gives you a way to escape. See, when you have no self-esteem and you don't love yourself, people will use you and walk over you and you feel like that is the way it is supposed to be. At the tender age of 19, and not knowing what tomorrow would bring, I turned to God. Despite all the things I had been through, my grandmother was praying for me. I may not have loved myself, but I knew God loved me. Yes, I questioned Him all the time about why I had to go through what I went through, but I also knew it was because of the choices that I had made. That same month, my son got sick and was admitted to the hospital. They did not know what was wrong, but he just had a high fever. We stayed there for two days. When I got home, my friend and her mother came over and told me I needed to go to church with them, as they were having a revival. That night the preacher taught on ways to escape and that God could bring you out of whatever problem you were in. I gave my life back to God and God dealt with me about what I was going through. One Sunday, the man of God preached a message, "You can't enter in like that." I told my children's father that we could no longer be together unless we were married and that was the worse fight we ever had. But because I felt I could not make it without him, I stayed. It was later I got the strength to leave.

After leaving him and getting up on my feet, I felt alone again. See, the devil knows your weakness and loneliness and feeling unwanted were mine. I let him back into my life, and this time it was not so much physical as it was verbal and emotional abuse. It went on for a couple of months. I was still changing personalities again to fit in wherever I was and whomever I was around. Well, he finally decided he wanted to be with some other girl, and we went our separate ways. Not long after that, I met another man. Once again, it all started out well. We dated for about a year, and he became very controlling. Yes, I took it because I still had no self-esteem, and because I thought bad love was still better than no love at all.

What I'm trying to say is because I'd never learned as a child who I was and how to love myself. I went into my adulthood feeling the same way. We ended up getting married and having a son together. After about nine years of marriage, I remember being asked one day, by our pastor, "Kayla, what do you like to do?" I had no clue what I liked because my life had been centered on and around making everyone else happy. We later got divorced, and because I still had not fallen in love with myself, I started looking for it in men and drinking. I'd met a man that was not good for me at all, changed again to fit into his company, and lost everything I had. After losing my home, I moved in with my sister for a week or two until I could get back on my feet. At this point you would think I'd have changed, but I went from man to man looking for myself.

It wasn't until I was in my forties that I learned how to love myself and find out who I was. This was not the easiest thing to do, but with God, I made it. God is able to keep you. There were many times I wanted to throw in the towel. God had to hide me from the enemy, even when the enemy was me! I was at a point I could not and did not want to face life anymore. My life was filled with disasters and chaos, but through it all He kept me and protected me and finally isolated me so I could see what I really needed—God. Many times, we feel we need other people to identify who we are when we really only need God.

He had to show me, me. In order for Him to get the best out of me, I needed to be put under a magnifying glass. I need to be processed. We sometimes think we have to search out the answers when the answers are right before us. Life is too short to live it through the eyes of others. I had to learn how to be me for myself.

God had to show me how to fall in love with me. In learning how to love Him, I learned how to love me. In loving me, I now can love others and know when I am being loved. I know what love really is, and I also know what love is not. Loving and respecting yourself is the first step toward wholeness. I am now waking in the fullness of God, fulfilling the things that He has called me to do. I am happily married to the love of my life who loves me for who I am, and I did not have to change myself. You can overcome your childhood trauma with God, no matter what you went through or had to endure. God is the way out of it all. I am a survivor, and you can be one too.

Shirley Lancaster, born to a 73-year-old father and a 49-year-old mother, began her humble beginnings in a rural, northern Louisiana community in the 60s. Due to their ages, the doctors recommended that her parents abort her because they falsely predicted that she would have Down's Syndrome.

In her memoir, Survive and Thrive Against the Odds, she talks about how the childhood traumas she experienced had a lifelong effect on her self-esteem, which led to her becoming pregnant and quickly married at 17. Through many trials of rearing three children as a widow, Shirley is thankful for her family, who encouraged her to be obedient to God's Word, stay focused, and pray in faith.

By taking heed, she attained a Bachelor of Science from Grambling State University and a Master of Science in Organization Development from American University. Her career entails teaching, writing, and mentoring others in Jesus Christ.

TRAUMA FOR ME AS A CHILD

Shirley Lancaster

I was born to elderly parents: my dad was 73 years of age, and my mother was about 49 when I was born. They had little education, but they were hard-working people who believed in God and providing for their family. My dad was a widower with 10 adult children, including two sets of twins. His eldest daughter was only three years younger than my mother. On the other hand, my mother was a widow with four adult children, which included her own set of twins.

After 20-plus years of their changed marital statuses, my parents met at a Methodist church convention. Over time, their relationship later developed into a romance. Since my father had children who were older than my mother's, he was a happy and mature empty-nester. My mother's grown children were still at home.

Although they confessed to being Christians, an unexpected thing occurred after a few years of their courtship. During my mother's menopausal stage, she discovered that she was with child. Unlike today, being unwed and pregnant was considered a disgrace before God and man.

However, because of their ages, the doctors recommended they should abort me because they predicted I would be a mongoloid baby. As I mentioned in my memoir, *Survive and Thrive Against the Odds*, on the scheduled morning of the abortion, my brother hitchhiked an almost two-hour ride to the hospital to stop my mother from having the procedure done. She was already prepped in the surgical ward when my brother arrived and begged her not to abort me, because of a hopeful dream he'd dreamed the night before.

Although my mother was heavily medicated, she listened intensely and changed her plans, deciding to keep her faith in God regarding my birth and wellbeing.

Early Childhood Traumas

As a result of my mother's continuous smoking during her pregnancy, she gave birth to a very small, wrinkled baby girl. Thankfully, I did not have mongolism as the doctors predicted. However, studies show that one in every five babies born to mothers who smoke during pregnancy has low birth weight.

My First Trauma: A Taste of Hellfire

Before my siblings relocated to another state, one of my favorite sisters was preparing a dish in a large pot on our gas stove. I was at the beginning stages of standing, and as I tried to get up,

I gripped her legs while she was stirring the hot soup in the pot. I might have scratched or pinched her while trying to get a grip, which caused her to lose her balance. The entire hot pot of liquids and its contents landed upside down on my small head. I sat there crying for several minutes before someone was brave enough to remove the pot from my head and pick me up carefully, due to the rawness of my skin.

Initially, the doctors predicted I would never have normal skin and hair due to the severity of the third-degree burns. Although it took my skin and hair an eon to recover, each time my parents brought me in for checkups, the doctors were astounded at the remarkable progress of my healing.

When I got older, I related my burn experience to the story about the three Hebrew boys, in the book of Daniel, Shadrach, Meshach, and Abednego, who were thrown into a fiery furnace because they refused to bow down and serve King Nebuchadnezzar. I recovered from the burns without any physical scars.

My Second Trauma: My Siblings' Departure

I was less than four years of age, but I vividly remember the loneliness I felt when my sisters left to join my brother in another state. As they packed their belongings, I cried. They promised they would visit, but I knew it would not be the same as us living under the same roof. Like I imagined, our wooden frame house didn't feel the same after their departure. I felt so alone in the countryside with my mother.

My Third Trauma: Daddy Is Dead

Since my parents were both farmers and landowners, they lived separately in different locations. It seemed like my only joyful hope was to look for my dad's faithful Wednesday evening visits. I anxiously stood on our enclosed veranda, awaiting the appearance of his shiny black car coming around the winding curve of the dirt road. He always brought me large Jackson cookies from the store he owned and managed in his small rural community. I glowed with joy when he picked me up, hugged, and kissed my forehead. Those were the best moments of each week, but the saddest moments each time he left to return to his house.

On one of my dad's visits, he asked my mother if I could go home with him. Thankfully, she consented. What I didn't know was that my dad had a special surprise for me. As we got closer to his house, he asked me to close my eyes. When we arrived, he told me to open them and I saw the most beautiful, white Shetland pony I had ever seen.

Before he had even stopped driving, I jumped out of the car so I could get closer to it. I couldn't believe my eyes. He had asked me on several occasions to tell him what I wanted. Of all things, I wanted a small horse rather than a doll, like most children my age.

He saddled the pony and placed me on it, and he walked along beside me down the dirt road and back. It was the heat of summer, so he and I were hot but happy.

The week went by quickly as he worked in the store each day. My math lessons initially started when my mother taught me how to count vegetable seeds, and they continued with my dad teaching me how to count money. His customers couldn't believe that an old man of 73 had a little girl. With adoration, they were very patient with my newly learned counting skills.

When my mother showed up on the weekend to bring me back to her home, I was so sad. I knew I would miss the love and fun times my dad had shown me day after day. He never got as distraught about things as my mother did, he was easy going.

My dad loved my mother's food, so before we departed, my mother prepared several meals for him that would last him throughout the week. As a matter of fact, everyone loved my mother's food—she was a natural.

Before we left, my dad would routinely check my mother's car to make sure it was operational and safe; neither one of them had new cars. While he was doing that, my mother enjoyed observing Dad's produce on his farmland. They always compared notes about their progress and knowledge, but to me it seemed more like a competition.

When we returned to her house, our routine continued as usual. We worked the farmland by pulling up weeds, planting seeds in the rows, and feeding the chickens, cows, and hogs. Although my dad had a farm and animals to feed, I never had to work. Instead, he allowed me to play.

The next Wednesday evening, my dad did not show up as usual. I waited a long time and looked out of the window until that night. I even got up in the middle of the night to see if I saw his shiny black car. When I unintentionally woke up my mother, she angrily cursed at me, and with tears in my eyes, I finally fell asleep.

Since we didn't have a telephone, the next morning my mother and I drove down to his home to see if he was okay. My mother was nervous and edgy. When we got closer to his home, she firmly commanded me to stay in the car until she came out to get me. I was so tempted to get out of the car and pet my pony, but I knew better.

She finally reappeared with an expression of sadness and dismay. When I jumped out of the car, I ran into the house and discovered my dad lying on his back porch covered with flies. I tried to shake him, but I knew he was dead. I wished I was dead with him.

My Fourth Trauma: My Dad's Funeral

Although my grandparents on my mother's side had both died while I was alive, I couldn't remember their funerals. They had died during the time my skin was very raw and tender. I was so sad at my dad's wake seeing him lying in the casket with his suit on and as stiff as a brick. I just wanted him to get up and hug me, as he always did.

One good thing happened that made me happy, and that was when my sisters and my brother came home—I was elated to see them again. My dad's funeral was held days later, down the road from his home, store, and my pony.

I tried to hold back the tears, but the longer I sat there listening to the songs and the people talking about my dad, the more difficult it was for me. Finally, it happened—an outburst of tears suddenly flooded my tiny face, and my heart felt like it would burst. Immediately, my aunt picked me up and carried me out of the church to get some fresh air.

What I couldn't understand was why God took my dad away from me. I was angry at God for doing that—it just didn't make sense to me.

My Fifth Trauma: School Integration

Throughout kindergarten and elementary school, I had made all As and a few Bs. Sadly, after integration, I discovered I wasn't as smart as I thought. The books at the Black school were outdated, and apparently, some teachers were too.

At the beginning of my fifth grade, I was one of the first Black students chosen to attend the White school. After my first year there, my life changed. I struggled academically and socially. I had challenges comprehending what I read. Because my mother valued education, she exempted me from farming duties on school days. Although I studied from the time I got home until the morning hours, I still struggled to master the information at a satisfactory level. The only time I took a break from studying and homework was when my mother called me to eat supper. I ate little and slowly due to having a nervous stomach. My mother was always very patient with me during our meals.

It wasn't until I had changed schools that I realized how much I missed the Black school environment, the students, and especially the teachers. The Black teachers were encouraging, more approachable, and personable. They knew my mother and my entire family, which was the complete opposite of the White teachers.

As a minority in a White school, I became conscious of my darker skin color and curly hair. During recess, I avoided the sun to prevent my skin from getting darker and because my mother put too much oil on my hair, which caused it to glisten and draw negative attention. Sometimes I would go into the bathroom and wipe as much off as I could to lessen the shine.

No matter how much I studied, it seemed like I made no progress. Due to my mother's lack of education, she couldn't assist me in my schoolwork. Disheartened, I was retained in the 5th grade, which was most embarrassing.

Lumsden (1997) suggests that a teacher's expectations play a crucial role in student performance. Higher expectations tend to increase the level of student performance. However, lower expectations allow students to work at a lower level even if they can produce higher-quality material. A teacher's attitude and expectations determine how hard a student strives to work during a specific academic year. Ornstein and Levine (1990) suggest another element of motivating students involves the teacher's expectations and perception of the student's ability to learn. Low teacher expectations can lead to a student's low performance. If the teacher perceives the student as an inadequate learner, the student, in turn, lives up to that expectation; this fosters a self-fulfilling prophecy. Other factors impacting motivation include a lack of success in earlier school experiences and negative peer pressure. The lack of success leads to the student's belief they are not a capable learner and have no chance to be successful in school.

I had many dreams as a child; some I remembered, while others vanished quickly. Yet, one stayed on my mind and came to pass. I dreamed my sister lived with us and it came to pass. Although this particular sister was the one who accidentally caused me to get burned, over time, she became my favorite sister. She was the only sibling who went to college. As she encountered the stresses of life in her marriage and environment, my mother encouraged her to leave the windy city of Chicago and return to our home. She was my ram in the bush. As a teacher, she helped me during the summer and soon discovered after looking at my notes that I needed glasses. As a result of the eye exam, the doctor determined that my vision was very poor due to a cataract in my left eye.

Thankfully, with vision correction and academic, spiritual, and moral support from my sister, I regained my title as an honor roll student. My past school agonies turned out as priceless blessings in a number of ways.

My Sixth Trauma: Physical Abuse and Depression

Jealousy consists of thoughts and feelings that show signs of insecurity and fear, and things were going too well for me. My mother was quite frugal due to having a small, fixed income, and although teachers didn't make enormous salaries, my sister made more money than my mother. Therefore, my sister afforded me more opportunities. She got me off of the free lunch plan at school, she took me with her to her hairstylist, we went shopping at malls for clothing, shoes, jewelry, and whatever else I wanted.

Needless to say, this new lifestyle did not make my mother too happy. In the past, my mother made my dresses and skirts for school, which were not stylish like the other girls' clothes. I was always embarrassed, but I didn't have a choice. My mother could only afford to buy me one or two pairs of shoes on credit at the only shoe store in our small hometown in northern Louisiana. One pair was for church and the other was for school, but my sister was able to buy me several colors of shoes to match my outfits.

When my mother got upset, she cursed both my sister and me, using many hurtful words. Any time she got angry with me she would say she should have aborted me while she had the chance. "Those doctors told me and your dad you wouldn't be normal, and they were right!" she would say. "You ain't been nothing but trouble ever since your black ass was born!" When I heard those words, I felt like a knife had pierced my heart and I was walking on eggshells. After mouthing off a few times too many, I finally learned not to because a serious beating would follow. When that happened, I wore long sleeves to cover the bruises and scars. My sister tried to reason with her, but it was to no avail—a few times, my mother tried to beat my grown sister. She was as frightened as me.

One day, as soon as I got in from school, my mother started fussing and cursing, saying many hurtful words to both my sister and me. So, I found about 80 of my mother's pills and took all of them. I don't know how long I was unconscious, but my sister found me hours later and rushed me to the emergency room. When I recovered consciousness, I was in the hospital, and my sister was praying for me. When asked by the medical staff why I had tried to take my life, I was too afraid to answer, but the unhealed bruises on my body answered for me.

Once home, I overheard my brave sister's serious conversation with my mother about the power of negative words. Surprisingly, my mother sat and listened calmly, without interruption. Deep down in my heart, I knew she was still very capable of going back to her normal self when she got angry. But the only thing she had to say to my sister—along with a few choice words—was this: "You have spoiled my child."

Although I was young, my heart was touched by my mother's sad expression. I knew that she meant well and didn't intentionally mean to hurt me. However, due to her lack of understanding and education, she only replicated what she had experienced in her youth.

Lessons Learned from Childhood Traumas

One thing my mother said when I didn't understand something was, "Just keep living." As I got older, many things became clearer, and I could relate to 1 Corinthians 13:11, NIV: "When I was a child, I spoke as a child, I understood as a child, I thought as a child; but when I became a man, I put away childish things."

Just as I couldn't choose my parents, I realized they did choose me. As I grew into a mature adult, I had opportunities and choices to make some changes. I asked myself some of the following questions, "Am I going to have a distasteful attitude toward God because He allowed me to be born to elderly, uneducated parents? Am I going to continue holding a grudge against God because my favorite parent died when I was only five years of age? Why were my parents' farmers when other parents had professional jobs? Why did I have a mother who seldom showed love and affection? Why were we black? Why did she beat me all the time instead of disciplining me by explaining the causes and effects of my behavior?" The questions could go on and on.

Although my family had many dysfunctional behaviors, I had to choose to either recognize the value of my upbringing and culture or dwell on the negatives, which would not get me where I needed to be in life. I later learned that they actually modeled priceless lessons of work ethic, land ownership, entrepreneurship, faith, money management, and perseverance, which aided me throughout life. When I became a parent, I made better choices with my children who are now faithful, God-fearing young adults and parents.

As a child, my parents' occupation as farmers didn't seem significant, but as an adult, I reflected on their efforts in producing organic food. Both of them, a widow and widower, reared their children during the era of the Great Depression, and I understood all of our lives are full of tribulation and distress. I examined my attitude and my choices, realizing that making the right choices often determined whether my life would go well or become difficult. As Proverbs 11: 4-6, NIV says "The righteousness of the blameless makes their paths straight, but the wicked are brought down by their own wickedness."

Whether we have these revelations early or late, it is up to the individual to do something about our discoveries. I consent with Paul in that God's decision to hide so many wonders from man is an act of love and a gift inside the process of life.

Rev. Lakisha L. Tucker M.S, B.A., B.S., LCAS-A is an Educator, Licensed Substance Abuse and Addiction Counselor (LCAS-A), and a Licensed Minister of the Gospel of Jesus Christ. Lakisha's passion is working with youth and their families. She comes from a long line of educators and it is important to her to continue to carry the torch. She believes that all children can go from students to scholars within their own abilities. She also understands the struggle that families face when addiction and abuse come into play.

Lakisha was born and raised in Greensboro NC, and reared in a single parent home along with her sister. She is a mother, wife, sister and friend. Lakisha learned early about hard work, determination, ethics, resilience, and tenacity. She graduated from Southeast Guilford High School in 1992.

Lakisha matriculated to North Carolina A&T State University (NCA&T SU) where she earned a degree in Psychology. She had a thirst for education and went back to obtain a degree in Special Education in 2004 (also from NCA&T SU). With the passion to serve people and help them fulfill their life's purpose, she received her Master's in Mental Health Counseling in 2013.

It was after a negative situation at her daughter's school that she became an author, writing her first children's book, I Just Want to be Me! She went on to write a memoir, A Sun's Journey and a journal, Learning to Thrive through Tough Transitions and, Daleeia's Oh No, Second Grade.

Lakisha is always working on her "next book!" She has been given the gift of poetry and has been called the "Author Extraordinaire." Lakisha has a blog on wordpress.com along with a popular story telling corner that she created during the pandemic "Kisha's Korner."

FROM TRAUMA TO TESTIMONY

Lakisha L. Tucker

When I was a child, for the most part things were pretty sweet. I enjoyed playing outside with my friends, roller skates, and my Pink Panther bike. It was beautiful; the bike actually had Pink Panther's face and was pink and white. The best part about my childhood was going to the skating rink once a week. I learned to speed skate and skate with one leg out to the side, squatting, and backwards. I thought I was the number one skater in North Carolina.

I also enjoyed the spring and summers. My cousins and I enjoyed playing at the park where everyone gathered. There was a basketball goal, merry-go-round, swings, and a little stream of water. We loved to play in the stream and tried to make that our first activity so our shoes had a chance to dry. We dared each other to jump the creek and sometimes there was a slip or two and the damage always showed on our shoes. No matter how many times we were warned by Granny, we always jumped the creek. Well, that was until my oldest cousin started getting in trouble (those were the days where the responsibility fell on the oldest sibling/

cousin). He soon discovered it was better to jump the stream with our shoes off!

Then there were Sunday dinners after church. We were lucky enough (because of poverty, but I never knew) to enjoy feasts with our extended family. There was always enough food to go around, no matter where we went. I was blessed enough to have on my hot plate fresh rolls, mac n cheese with the big noodles, collards, spicy cabbage, roast chicken, and much more.

Then there were the weekends where I enjoyed country living with my cousins. They lived about thirty minutes away, where the air seemed to smell different. There were trees for days and more yard to play in than any apartment complex. We had the best breakfast there after we cleaned up on Saturday, and we walked to church afterward.

My life seemed like a coin that was left in the change compartment in a car where one side was exposed to everything sticky. That side got stuck to everything else left behind, while the top was exposed to very little and still exhibited the luster of its shine.

A Life of Trauma

From birth, my life was traumatic. I was born with some deformities, extra fingers, and crossed eyes. I was also born into a family of dysfunction. My mother was a young one and my alcoholic father abused her. It was as if I was doomed from day one. We were poor, Black, and in America. The chances of success seemed slim.

I remember lying on my mother's lap as she was on the phone, while my father was yelling and screaming outside and trying to break down the door. I cannot remember what triggered this memory, but when I asked my mom about it, she believes I was about three when this event happened. Secondly, my mother and I always seemed to be hiding. We were living by the mall with a lady that had multiple cats at the time. When we exited the car one day, she grabbed my hand and said, "Your father is hiding under that bush; we are going to walk back to the car." Lastly, somehow things got twisted up at the school and instead of my cousin picking me up, I was put on the bus. Because of my father's past behavior, they thought he'd kidnapped me. My family had gone to the house looking for me and I was not there. Baffled as to where I could be, they called the police. Little did they know hours beforehand I had gotten off the bus and one of the neighbor's grandmothers yelled out and asked if I wanted to come to her house for a little while and play. Of course, I could not pass that up. It seemed like a sweet idea as I would not be home alone, and there would be a hot meal and friends. My family did not agree. I was found when they began going house to house, knocking on doors to see if someone had seen me. I came around the corner smiling.

What I am learning about childhood trauma is that it is a nasty root that grows and festers. If it is not killed, you take those same traumatic situations into your adult life and relationships. This trauma continues to grow and grow. Welcome to my life! I did not know what I was getting in to.

On warm summer days, my friends and I enjoyed the run of the recreation center. We played games, played outside on the metal slides that were HOT, played basketball, softball, ping pong, and made up our own cheers. Our favorite, c-h-e-e-r-l-e-a-d-e-r-s, oh yes, we are the best! CHEERLEADERS. We went back and forth from the center to our house, and one day as we walked to the recreation center, we stopped at the grocery store. We had collected enough cheerwine bottles to turn them in for cash at the grocery store. Some of my friends wanted to walk around the store, deciding on chips and other junk food. What we would find would change my life for a lifetime.

As we rounded the corner, we saw a young gentleman that spoke after we came from the bathroom. He was stocking the refrigerated section of the store. He turned around and asked, "How old are you?" I replied, "Ten, why?" He told me I was too young and asked if I had an older sister. I told him about my mother in my innocence. I regretted that day for years to come. Really, for the rest of my life. I introduced them.

It wasn't long before they were dating and my mom was pregnant, and shortly afterwards they were married. It had always been my mom and I in the home and all of a sudden, things changed. He was in the home all day and night. Now there were two children and at almost eleven I was responsible for my baby sister. It was like I stepped into the role of being her surrogate mother. Before cell phones we used home phones and I wanted to go spend time with my friends. In order for me to do that, I had to take her with me because he was either sleep or drunk. I packed her bag and threw her on my hip and walked to my friend's house. It seemed that it took us forever to get there, but in actuality it was no more than a half of mile or so.

The Grooming Begins

Knock, knock, knock . . . don't answer the door. The fear of panic came over me. In our neighborhood, once you got home, did your homework and chores, you were free to go play. My mind boggled and I couldn't figure out why he would say NO! By this time, my friends were standing under the balcony yelling, "Can Kisha come outside?" I turned and repeated the question and was given the same response: NO. I was frightened because by this time he was telling me to come here as he sat with bended knees on the floor.

He asked if I had ever had a massage. At ten years old, I didn't know what a massage was or how it happened. He waves me over to position me on the floor and massaged me. He rubbed up and down my back, the first time. Each time after that, he progressed as to what he touched and how he touched. He slowly ran his hands down the spin of my back. By this time, he was using oils/lotions to caress me.

One particular time, I had to ask him to take me to a friend's house. My mom asked him to give me money to go to the mall with my friends. On the drive over in his long blue car, I sat in the backseat. He wanted to play a game with me guessing which hand the ten-dollar bill was in or the twenty-dollar bill. I can remember guessing wrong and almost cringing. Now, I felt like I had to grovel at his feet to beg for the bigger bill. I begged and pleaded with him to give me the twenty-dollar bill, but he was insistent and said no with a sinister laugh. I exited the car feeling defeated, walking into the sleepover with my head down. I knew if we went to the mall that I would be the one with the least amount of money. The massages didn't stop. He then involved my cousin, and in my eyes, it couldn't be wrong what he was doing and where his warm moist hands would land.

There are certain things I will never forget, the smell of his private stock of beer in the green funny shaped bottle, the prickly feel of a mustache and beard, and the feeling of helplessness. He never asked me not to tell, I was paid to keep quiet. Not necessarily with money, but with gifts from the store, letting me go outside, and providing protection from the neighborhood bullies.

Finally, I'm Free

Tiffany and I had a sleepover, and we did what most girls do. We played all day, laughed, and giggled. At bedtime, her mom came to the door, said goodnight, and cut off the light. We shared our secrets. It was strange that I was first because we never got to her secret now that I think about it. I shared with her that my stepfather was having oral sex with me, kissing and fondling me, and masturbating in front of me.

It was finally out, and I didn't know if I had done the right thing or not. I recall her yelling out to her mom to come into the room. I glanced at her with fear in my eyes and said, "You said you wouldn't tell!" Her mom reassured me everything was fine, and I was safe. Tiffany looked at me and said, "That's not right, he's not supposed to do that to you."

The next morning was a whirlwind. When we woke up, the police were there, and all the questions began. I felt like I told that story repeatedly. It was like I was a broken reel in a movie theater that kept playing the same movie. Better yet, a GPS that continues to say REROUTING. I wanted to go home at this point, but repeatedly I was told I couldn't right now. Several people revolved through the door from morning to evening, and I stayed another night. I could finally go home, and it was odd. My mother asked me why I didn't tell her. I didn't know why, but I felt like I had destroyed a utopian society and I was the black sheep. Over the next few days, social workers came to my school, I was pulled from class, and expected to talk. They came to my home and I was expected to talk. I thought, "How many times can I tell you the same story? How many times can I show you where it happened and the how?" I regretted I had ever said a word. The only thing that ever benefited me was that he was not there and not molesting me anymore.

When I Thought I was Safe

When I thought I was safe, I learned he had been arrested. I was relieved! Then I was bamboozled again. He was coming BACK. Supposedly, there were rules to this whole reentry thing, but I was the only one following the rules. He returned and was not to be left alone with me. WELL, HE WAS! To recapture one event, he entered my room where I had my sister with me, and he said, "Give her something to keep her quiet." She was given potato sticks, and I asked him to hurry as my sister watched him molest me. He finished and found his way to the couch and began to masturbate. He asked if I wanted to watch, and I replied I just wanted to make sure my sister was okay. He masturbated and went to work as if this were normal. It was a cycle, and I was caught up in the middle of a vicious wheel. Now the story had a different ending, and it been dredged up again.

When he left this time, he was gone for good, and things really changed. We went from going to the five-dollar store every week to having our power cut off or notes left on the door. I thought things were bad then, but they went from worse to atrocious. If I felt like the black sheep before, I really felt like the black sheep then. The self-esteem I had was gone, the thrive to live was gone, and the zeal to live a successful like was gone. Who could love a girl like this? I was dirty, used up, and angry he didn't have sex with me to finish the deal. That's when I asked him the question, "Why didn't you just have sex with me?" The response was stiffening: "Oh, I could never do that!" I said with my twelve-year-old mind, "You might as well; there is not much left." I was unaware of what my body was doing, as he touched me, and how it felt so right, but was so wrong. How I could enjoy something that made my stomach turn and made me want to vomit?

My final thoughts on my childhood trauma:

Did I Give You Permission To Make Me Cry?

Did I give you permission to make me cry?

I'm left asking myself, why?

Why do you think it's okay to groom me
to be a bride of gloom?

I have no control over what you say or do,
it's only for you.

I just want to be a child; one that likes to play and run
around wild.

To feel the breeze as it blows from the trees
and runs around scraping my knees.

Now, I'm wondering if you would do it today or if I
would be able to play with my friends outside?

Or if I would need to wash in peroxide
to get the filthy feeling of you off me?

I just really want to be a kid, you see.

I didn't give you permission to make me cry,

but now I understand why God spared my life, even with
all the strife.

There were nights that the enemy played with my mind.
The thoughts he sent were not kind.

I thought about taking my life,
because it didn't have a valued price.

Thank God my help was a phone call away.
God really sent an angel that day.

Now, I know why the devil wanted to kill ME. He could
see what God had in store for me.

Devil, what you sent to kill ME
only made ME stronger.

They say the race is not given to the swift nor to the
strong, but to he that endureth until the end.

You made ME cry, but in the END, I WIN

The devil will always set you up to kill, steal, or destroy you. I have
decided that he doesn't get that right, not anymore, not in my life.

Oh No, Not Again

Oh no, not again

Isn't this a sin?

I can hear him coming

I wonder will I ever win?

I wish I had the courage to say stop

But instead, I freeze, and my heart drops.

All the time in my mind I'm screaming

Leave me alone!

As he moans and groans.

It's finally over,

I feel like such a pushover.

Why couldn't I open my mouth

Or be as strong as a mammoth?

The next time, I will be ready

And before he gets all sweaty,

I will have the courage to say

Stop . . . My body doesn't belong to you.

I'm just a little girl.

When I hurl those words into his face,

He will leave my room like a horse in a race.

I finally did it, I got courage with God's grace.

Sadly, I can never erase,

The feelings of shame and guilt,

That have me bound to the past

Built on pain

I finally realized I was not to blame!

God has shown me that there will be a purpose for my pain.

He will give me BEAUTY for ASHES.

To my children, please forgive me for clinging too close. I hope I didn't love too hard. I apologize for having to know their parents before you could stay. All I ever wanted to do was to keep you safe.

Charlene Yuvette Atchison was born in Buffalo New York, but now resides in Erie Pennsylvania. She attended Bennett High School and Buffalo State College to pursue an Associate Degree in Child Psychology.

She is the author of her first book Chronicles of Being Adopted followed by Releasing The Pain, My Inner Thoughts, and Shattered But Still Standing. She is also a contributing author of the anthology, Women Overcome Through Writing (WOW) and When Healing Hurts: Living Through the Loss of a Loved One. She has also contributed to two Poetry books.

Charlene is the proud mother of two adult daughters and a grandmother as well. Her vision is for others to see that they are not alone and by reading her books, they will understand that, "God will bring you through everything that you go through."

NOT A DADDY'S GIRL

Charlene Atchison

Every little girl wants to be daddy's girl, the apple of her father's eye, and the one her daddy tells everyone is his baby girl. Every little girl wants to have that strong bond with her father, the man that will protect her no matter what, the man that will hurt anyone that hurts her. What a wonderful feeling that is when a little girl feels secure knowing her daddy loves her.

Life started changing for me at a very young age and it was all at the hands of the man I called "Daddy" which was the man who was supposed to protect me from all hurt, harm, and danger. This man decided that he would be the one to cause me the hurt that I carried into my adulthood.

The pain I felt as an adult while dealing with childhood trauma is beyond words at times. I tried for years to move on, but for some reason, the trauma always lingered in the back of my mind.

Why me, God? Why on earth would you allow this to happen to me? What did I do that was so wrong that my "dad" would take away my virginity? As much as I prayed for an answer, it was years before God answered me. I had to understand that God was there with me the whole time, and what took place was a part of my purpose in life. In order to tell people that they can overcome childhood sexual abuse, you have to know what that feels like. In order to walk in forgiveness, you have to forgive your abuser.

Knowing that I would never be that Daddy's little girl was so hard for me to deal with, but I finally accepted the fact he was sick and what was done to me was beyond wrong and there was no way for us to have a father/daughter relationship because he didn't see me as his daughter. I had to come to the understanding that the love I needed from my dad couldn't be given, and at some point, I would have to move on with my life and find a way to let this trauma go.

See, for years I wore this "mask" on my face that had a fake smile and pretended that everything was alright. I pretended that it had never happened until one day I found myself in a situation that caused me to relive what was done to me as a child and all these flashbacks hit me at once and I was forced to deal with what was done to me. I was forced to deal with the fact that I was diagnosed with depression and Bipolar disorder along with anxiety issues. I was forced to say "I need help NOW" after trying several times to take my life.

Dealing with the hurt and shame that I carried was so hard, especially when the people that I did tell didn't believe me due to who my "dad" was. I felt rejected because no adult wanted to be the one to say, "Hey, something needs to be done." The crazy part is I know I am not the only that has experienced people not believing them. They said I had made it up to get attention, yet years later what I said then is the same statement I am making now. So, it made sense to me to just act as if all was well with me.

I came to the understanding that in order for me to move past the hurt and shame of being molested, I would have to forgive my "dad" before he asked for my forgiveness, which he finally did a few years before he passed. I had to forgive him in order to move on with my life, but I also had to forgive myself. Why? Well, because God told me to. I know that might sound crazy to some, but I remember the day He told me it was time to forgive and let go. I questioned myself and really thought I was going crazy, but I knew deep down it was time to walk into forgiveness. I prayed and asked God to give me a forgiving heart towards my "dad" and He did that. Now, it didn't happen overnight. It took a while, but I am grateful that it did. Then God said it was time for me to forgive myself. I had to forgive myself for allowing the childhood trauma to control my life.

I was ready to live my life in complete peace and not allow what I went through as a child to control my life in the way that it was. Now, don't get me wrong, I went through many stages of dealing with forgiving the man, but as I look back on it now, the freedom that I feel is amazing. I now have a voice that can speak up against childhood sexual abuse. I have a voice that can say, "I know how you feel and this is how I was able to deal with it." I have a voice that can speak on behalf of other children who can't speak up right now for themselves.

I have family members who still don't believe me and they have that right; we don't speak anymore and I have learned to be alright with that, but I am thankful I am living in my truth and that I can share my story. Sharing what took place in my life for others to read and judge is not easy, but if it helps one person, then it was all worth it.

I am thankful for the opportunity to share my story and to share how I have overcome it. My sincere prayer is that my story will be a complete blessing to someone and they will know without a doubt they are not alone.

Cammie Stateman-Pitts has an ever-pressing mandate on her life to disseminate vital information. Whether it is to people about the importance of their lives, or customers about their services, or even to military families regarding benefits they are entitled, she believes, "people should be in the know."

She has been active in ministry since 1992. Mentoring, counseling, and encouraging people is one of her passions. People need to know; they are deeply and unconditionally loved and have great purpose in life.

Another passion was her business, established in 2000, CLS' Coordinations. She had been coordinating events years prior. However, it was not until a dream; that she became both inspired and believed she could be an entrepreneur. She takes her clients' vision and gives it life.

For approximately nine years, she was a "Certified" Army Family Team Building Instructor (AFTB) for various Army Reserve units.

Cammie is married, has two adult children, and four grandchildren.

A Passion to Forgive

Cammie Stateman-Pitts

There are some of us that have and will experience certain unfortunate and/or unacceptable happenstances/maltreatment during our young and/or adult lives. I now believe those of us who have been the victim of such experiences need not remain a victim if we do not want to. But we can utilize the experiences to motivate us to become victoriously free in mind, body, and spirit. The adage "it takes a village to raise a child" remains true today. Furthermore, and fortunately, it takes a lot more than finances to raise a child. I am a strong believer in that it takes a plethora of things. Among the most vital in my opinion are the caregiver('s) presence, love, attention, affirmation, and protection. Not necessarily in that order, but necessary nonetheless.

I was taught there were certain taboos; that is, certain topics that were never to be discussed. A strongly believed and enforced saying was; "What happens in my house or in the family, stays within the house or within the family." Consequently, there were a lot of "family secrets" and because of those secrets, countless children like me unnecessarily suffered in silence. I have experienced a lot of different childhood abuses and traumas: physical, emotional, sexual, and psychological. However, I found liberty in seeking God out and building a relationship with Him. I discovered that in receiving God's unconditional love, comfort, and peace, I was relieved and empowered with knowledge, peace, and the desire to, over time, truly forgive all my abusers. I came to understand forgiveness is not a weakness but a strength. The value of forgiveness is priceless and the cost equally so. In my journey to forgive, forgiveness catapulted me towards the healing process. I learned forgiveness did not mean the abuser's actions were condoned. Over time, the power in me forgiving healed relationships that otherwise would have been lost. I cannot overemphasize that forgiveness is a process. It begins with "ME" wanting to be free and me dealing with me.

I aspire to share with you some incidents that took place while I lived with my great-aunt and uncle in New York. I lived with them for about 10 years. In the course of that time, I went back and forth between New York and New Jersey, visiting my family.

Mind you, my siblings thought I was living the life given that my uncle was a manager for an Ideal Toy store. They were so captivated by me having access to all the toys a child could want that seemingly nothing else mattered when they came to visit me. How completely wrong they were.

After giving birth to three sons, my mother yearned for a daughter. Her desire became a reality; I was born 11 months after the birth of my third brother. What was puzzling to me was why she gave me up at the tender age of two to live with my aunt? This question was not answered until decades later, around 1993.

I was married to an army solider, and we relocated to New Jersey in 1992. Even though my mother and I had not spent a lot of mommy-daughter time together or built our mother-daughter relationship like the average mother and daughters, I knew my mother loved me and I loved my mother. Yet something was amiss with our relationship.

By now, all of my mother's children were adults. So, she became a foster parent. As time passed, my mother and I spent a lot of time together. I noticed I felt a certain way around her. Every time I saw her engage with other children and show them the love I felt I did not receive, it did something to me. The issues with my mother became worse and worse until one day I blurted out, "Why didn't you do that for me? I am your biological daughter and you did not do that for me!"

The next day, my mother and I sat down and had a heart-to-heart talk. We talked for hours. During our conversation, my mother found out a lot of things. She would interject from time to time, "I did not know, I just did not know." At first the anger came out through sarcasm, which was odd for me. I quickly realized that was the hurt speaking. I was raised to respect my parents and elders, or else. As I shared with her the horrific details of incident after incident, tears flowed from her eyes, and she hung her head in disbelief. My mom became very sorrowful. After I finished, she explained to me her strategy and struggle back then was for her and the boys to survive.

My mom reminded and shared with me some of the terrible abuse she and my brothers underwent at the hand and mouth of my dad.

I quickly became remorseful and so very ashamed. I remember how he was. I thought, "How selfish of me?" I felt so bad. I apologized to her for thinking ill of her and having the attitude I had. My aunt had lied to both of us the entire time. You see, my mother thought it would be advantageous for me to live with my aunt and uncle in New York, seeing how they were financially well-to-do. My aunt owned several businesses. Even though my mother was a nurse and my dad was a road construction foreman, my family lived destitute because my dad was an alcoholic, a gambler, and a womanizer. He was also very verbally, physically, and emotionally abusive to all of us. Besides, as a teenager, my mother had stayed with my aunt a couple of summers without incident. Therefore, at the time, my mom could not see the harm in letting me live with my aunt. Not to mention my aunt literally begged my mom to let her take me. The understanding was I would stay until the situation with my dad changed for the better. My aunt also promised I would get a good education. In my case it was a parochial school, Our Lady of Lords.

The physical abuse from my aunt began, perhaps around four or five years old. I remember being around five and learning how to clean a house according to my aunt's instructions and expectations. By age six, I knew how to clean the house. For example, I had to use a toothbrush, a bucket of soapy water and a cloth to clean the living-room floor. My aunt was a perfectionist, to say the least. She showed me one time how to handle and wash something and then if I did it wrong or missed an area I was slapped in the face and yelled at. If I continued to get it wrong, I would get slapped in the face a couple more times while being yelled at and hit in the head, grabbed by my arm, and shaken.

The situation would always escalate quickly. By then I was so scared I would end up forgetting what she initially showed me. I would be so afraid of getting a beating with the dog's stick. You see, my aunt had a golden retriever and she would beat him with the stick when he got out of hand or did something wrong. I do not mean a twig or switch. I mean a branch off a tree that she would strip of leaves. I remember the stick being bigger than me at that time.

In any case, I more than likely was put on punishment. I was usually slapped in the face, hit on my head, and/or beat with the stick. The beatings with the stick were much worse when she told me to go take a bath, as my skin would be softer after a bath. I was always scared I would do something wrong or miss a spot, or worse, break something.

Once a month we would clean what she called her wet-knots. These were an array of figurines and small sculpted objects like little souvenirs she'd collected or received as gifts throughout her life. She stressed that some of them were expensive, very valuable, and others were priceless. You can imagine the fear I had when I kept breaking some. I tried to hide one or two, but she knew where every one of them was supposed to be and would ask me. She would use the stick to beat me, stating I was trying to be sneaky. She said all I had to do was be honest and tell her, but since I was trying to deceive her, I was asking for a beating.

Oh, the beatings I would get for misspelling my name. I hated my name because while I was learning how to spell it, I would always leave out the second M. I often wondered why my first name had to have two Ms. We would go over spelling my name, and as usual, the lesson would include slaps, hitting me in the head, and yelling at me. There were times she would curse me out, call me names, and compare me to my siblings in negative ways. She frequently argued with me about my mom and dad and their situation.

In addition to any physical discipline, I was also punished by sitting on a commercial sized-plastic roll, which stood 2 to 2.5 feet tall. It was placed in the kitchen corner. There my aunt could see me at all times when I sat on it. Oh, but you do not understand. I could not speak or play, only sit all day. I would sit on the plastic roll for days and days and days. And those days turned into weeks at a time. I could only get up to use the bathroom, go to school, or go to bed. I would even have breakfast, lunch, and dinner sitting on the plastic roll, holding my bowl or plate. When on punishment, I could not speak with my mother.

Over the course of ten years, you could count on both hands how many times I spoke with my mom on the phone. Which was a question I posed to her when we talked. I said to her, "You mean to tell me you never thought it odd that I was nearly always was on punishment whenever you called? After all that time, you did not suspect something was off?" She answered, "No."

Another form of punishment was to lock me in the basement for what seemed like hours. My aunt owned a brick-face, which was a four-story apartment building. We resided on the entire first floor. That being said, you can now imagine how big the basement was. It had three separate rooms to it. The basement was dark and damp. I would cry profusely and bang on the door, pleading with her to let me in. She would respond by saying, "No, you are going to learn to obey me/do as I say."

My aunt only catered to my uncle. In other words, when we went food shopping, we would only get foods that he or she liked. There was nothing that I liked at all and of course there were no sweets, oh except for Breyer's peach ice cream. He loved it, so my aunt made sure there was plenty of Breyers in the freezer. I tried it, but did not like it at all. One day, my aunt was making a sandwich with some head cheese. The smell back then is the same even now: nasty. I told my aunt I did not want any. She made me a head cheese sandwich anyway and tried to make me eat it. I kept telling her, "No thank you, no thank you, I do not want it." She told me I could not eat anything else until I finished the sandwich. Furthermore, I was to sit on the plastic roll until I changed my mind. Seven days passed, and I ate nothing. I was so hungry and was about to give in until she showed me the sandwich was now stale. The bread was hard. She explained how lucky I was that the bread was stale. She offered me the usual for breakfast that day; raisin bran cereal. I hated the raisins as they stuck to my teeth. That was my uncle's favorite cereal, so that was the only type of cereal in the house.

I remember once when I was a third grader, my aunt and uncle went out drinking for the night with another couple. I went with them, but stayed in the car the entire night. I was told, "Under no circumstance get out of the car!" Even though I had to use the bathroom, I dared not get out the car because I knew what fate would befall me. So, I prayed I would go to sleep, and I did. When I woke up, they were walking towards the car, drunk and loud.

Another incident in particular that had a profound effect on me was when I was in kindergarten and we were allowed to wear our favorite clothes to school. I wore a red and mustard yellow plaid dress. The dress had pleats below the waist and a big mustard yellow bow tied on the top right side. It was my favorite dress. I am not sure how I got a stain on it. But when I return home, my aunt saw the stain. She was extremely upset with me. Not only did she beat me with the stick, but she made me take a bath then she beat me. In addition, she made me wear the dress for the remainder of the week to school with the stain on it. At the end of the week, my aunt had me wash the dress by hand with a washboard, even though she had a washing machine.

For as long as I can remember, my aunt would not allow me to play with other kids. It was strictly forbidden. I had no social life with kids my age. Her reason was, "They are bad kids and I do not want you around them." So, I played by myself most of the time, even though I had all the latest girl toys. It was boring playing alone. I would jump rope alone while four houses down from my house, five or six girls were having fun jumping double-dutch. A type of jumping rope I never learned because I was not permitted to interact with them. Sometimes I would sit outside and see the other kids playing hopscotch, jumping rope, double-dutch, hide and go seek or 1, 2, 3 red light. I just sat on the stoop and watched the other kids have fun and cried because I wanted to play with them.

Frequently, I felt alone, lived in fear, dread, and was afraid to tell my mother or anyone what was going on. The hardest time to keep silent were the times my mom visited me. The reason for my silence was because my aunt threatened to beat me with the stick if I told. My aunt said my mother was having enough problems and I would only cause her more problems. The worst lie my aunt told me was "your mom does not love you" and she said that was why I was with her. I dare not, even to this day, tell my dad about any of these things.

When my aunt was sober, she was cold, disconnected, and mean. For as long as I can remember, my aunt rarely showed me any kind of love. My uncle had little to say in raising me. He did not discipline me. He noticed I was usually on punishment. He would ask my aunt, "What did she do now?" We would speak, but we rarely talked except when he asked me to get his slippers from under the bed. I did not feel he was someone I would/could trust to ask for help.

Some may ask how I feel about my aunt and uncle today? Although both my aunt and uncle have passed away, I found closure in forgiving them and started the healing process in 1988. I learned that in order to receive forgiveness from God, I had to forgive my aunt and uncle and work on myself. I had to forgive myself and dispel the notion things were my fault, I brought the maltreatment on myself, and that I deserved the maltreatment. I want to emphasize forgiveness and healing was and is a process.

I wanted to ask my aunt why she treated me the way she did. I wanted to ask her if she had any regrets. The opportunity did come. My mother and I went to visit her in the hospital. When I walked into the hospital room, she immediately looked at me and told me to leave. She said she did not have anything to say to me and requested I leave. She passed away a few weeks later. I was hurt and did not understand her stance. I was relieved I did not base or delay my healing on waiting to speak with her. I am grateful for the wise counsel informing me of the possibility she could be hostile, in denial, and/or blame me. When I saw her, I thought I would cringe or be filled with fear. When I saw her for the first time after so many years, I did not hate her or want revenge. I felt sorry for her. That was when I knew that I had truly forgiven her.

I dedicate my writings to my Lord and Savior Jesus Christ without whom there would be no sane, healthy, whole me. Next, I thank my mother, who was my best friend and whose love taught me many things, specifically, the meaning of strength. Then, my children and grandchildren, who were and remain my greatest achievements. Last, my current husband Paul, who has demonstrated God's love and support through his love for me.

Belinda Strother is a mother of five adult children and four wonderful Grandchildren! She has a Master of Elementary Education and has been teaching English internationally for the past seven years.

Belinda is needy and suffers from Abandonment Issues! She was married for twenty years, got divorced about three years ago and has been trying to date since the beginning of this terrible Pandemic. She began to realize that every guy disappointed her simply by not texting or calling enough. She knew that they weren't dating and they technically didn't owe her much but she still felt empty and soulless by their lack of attention. What she figured out was that she craved acceptance! She is 54 years of age and still recovering from Childhood Trauma and Abuse!

Welcome to her journey!

THE MIRROR

Belinda Strother

The woman inside the mirror is in love with life. She is a loud laugher, a great listener, and has a fabulous smile. Her smile calms the wild waves of any body of water. That smile mesmerizes the men worthy enough to be graced by it. She is a sassy one that loves wearing hot pink shoes with matching nails of glitter. This woman is grateful for the people who were in her life for only a season because they were placed there for a reason. She sees my treasure, my jewel, my sweet lil girl looking back at her, but knows that the lil girl can't see her yet. The woman in the mirror with the pink shoes and the smile of gold desperately tries to get her attention from inside the mirror. The woman inside the mirror reaches out to my lil girl; she wants to touch her flawless brown face and hold it between her hands. She wishes to tell the lil girl that life does get better. Life will be better! She will be the woman she dreams of being. She will be brave, intelligent, beautiful, and hardworking, like her mother. She will be sassy and sweet, family oriented and unforgettable like her grandmothers. She will be warm, loving, adventurous, and creative, like her aunts. The woman wishes she could smash this mirror so she can touch the lil girl and reassure her it is okay to fight! Fighting is not common in her family of peacekeepers. To fight means to exhibit anger and show deep emotions, which is something she isn't familiar with. Her familiar role is to smile, be pleasant, and not cause any attention to be drawn to herself. The woman inside the mirror stifles a smirk because she knows what is within that soon-to-be feisty, unashamed, and unrelenting hot pink mess! She knows that my lil girl's future is full of adventure, peace, joy, and love. She will be a concoction of Dorchester badness, a little sourness, but mostly sweetness resulting in a fascinating trifecta! In the meantime, my innocent lil girl only sees her most hidden thoughts and feelings. She doesn't see the queen to be like I do. She doesn't see the woman in the mirror always watching, always hoping, always reaching out her hand for the lil girl to grasp.

A mirror catches a reflection in time; it does not care how you feel or what you look like. That mirror is going to reflect on what you present to it. Unlike a deep dark and disturbing secret, you really cannot hide from the truth, from reality, or from YOU when looking into a mirror. Do you know who you are? What do you see in the mirror? Is it pleasing to your eyes? Do you think your ancestors would approve?

I see you, lil girl, with your beautiful brown skin that you can't appreciate just yet because society tells you that White is right! Between society's limitations and your plight in life, your magic isn't allowed to flourish, but I believe in you. I have been here with you all along. I was here on the blessed day that you were born into this world. I have been here making sure that you survive, for you have a destiny.

Your bubbly breasts were passed down from your grandmother, whom you always wanted to be just like: spicy and sassy. The interesting thing is they bring a different kind of attention that you both enjoy and hate! It's no wonder self-doubt and shyness induce extreme discomfort in the presence of adult males. What are they looking at with that gross smile and glazed over devilish eyes? You wonder if they are in love with you, since that is what love is supposed to look like. Those cute and short bowlegs you must have inherited from your grandfather, because he always reminds you of a penguin waddling around. You wear that shape-fitting red mini dress because deep down inside of that beautiful mind you just want to be normal and noticed but not noticed simultaneously. My clueless lil pearl, when will you see that you are valuable? When will you learn to love yourself unconditionally? When will you forgive yourself for things you couldn't control?

The sun loves your legs with golden melanin and when you flash that beautiful smile, passed down from your momma, your ancestor's gasp, but you don't know that. You don't know your worth yet. I see the smile that hides your truth, uncomfortable in your own skin but yearning for that "pssst, hey girl" that lets you know you are sexy and acceptable. All the while your heart patters, your palms sweat, and you flash that signature smile as you wonder if your nose will betray you, mortify you, and possibly reveal the real you! Imperfectly damaged and hollow. I see you, lil girl, hiding in the corner with that mirror to your face as if you need a hit of cocaine. Mirror, mirror in my hand, am I still beautiful? Nope, no boogers there, thank God, because you know what it feels like for a guy to reject you, to say, "Shit, no I don't know that bitch!" You know what it feels like to see the light-skinned, longer-haired, bigger booty girl get all the attention—the attention you so desperately crave. You crave the attention of random strangers but cringe and retreat once your wish has been granted. Daddy issues much? Social anxiety anyone?

I see you, lil girl, and I so wish you could remember your childhood. I wish you remembered your childhood as happy and carefree. I wish you remembered that time when you were five years old, or that time when you were seven years old, or what about the time when you were nine or ten years old? No? My poor lil girl, you don't remember much at all. Has your mind been so protective of you that it erased YOU? Why can't you remember your childhood? Do you really need to remember when you were happy, sad, or indifferent? Who taught you how to ride a bike for the first time? How did you feel? Well, there was that red tricycle you had, but you only remember that because you saw yourself on it in a picture. Does that count as a memory? I know the few memories that are clear you wish you could forget, but that's not how life seems to work for you, my sweet girl. Will the memories flood back one day and drive you completely up and over the insanity mountain? You have climbed that mountain halfway several times, but your family was always there to catch you when you rolled head over heels back down; down to pain, down to pleasure, down to hell!

My lil girl, I have watched you ponder whether it was normal or important to not have many memories of your childhood to share with friends. It has weighed heavily on your mind because you wanted to be included in those girl chats that were full of laughter and fun. You were always so quiet, such a little imposter, trying to be one of the girls. I wonder if this is when you learned how to smile without truly smiling? Is this when the imposter was formed? Is this when your Frankenstein's monster was born? I see you, lil girl, searching for what every other little girl had. You wanted a life, a story to share that wouldn't chase the faint of heart away. You wanted a reason to run outside to tell your friends about the funniest thing that happened last night. Instead, you sit and smile and pretend to enjoy all the life happening around you as your Frankenstein's monster sits in wait because her time is coming! Do you know who you are? What do you see in the mirror? Is it pleasing to your eyes? Do you think your ancestors would approve?

What you do remember are feelings of fear, the prying hands, the uncomfortable questions, and the guilt. I know you aren't sure why you feel guilty, but what you do know is that men are the enemy! The fear, distrust, and constant feeling of doom when alone with the one you loved and hated was so confusing! Always, a tornado of emotions whipping my sweet lil girl around the guilt, around the fear, around the sadness, around the shame, around the confusion of the two Ps of pain and pleasure. The lil girl in the mirror was learning what love was not supposed to be like—at times fun and full of adventure and at times scary, dark, and despairing!

You never really hated him, you just wanted him to stop! You just wanted to be normal! You just wanted to live! The lil girl looks for her voice. Somewhere! Anywhere! She is thrown into the murky water, instructed to swim: swim, lil girl! Swim! But the fear, the fear is too strong. It takes control of her mind and tells her it is too late; you are done for! Just give up, give in and die! Die like they did in the movie that haunts you to this day! All bloody and mangled, shredded, and ripped limb from limb! Scream, my lil girl! Scream for all the pain and pleasure! Scream for all the days, nights, afternoons, and times when you couldn't BE! Scream for the YOU that was so cruelly stolen from you! Scream, lil girl! Who are you? Look into that damn mirror and decide! Decide to live! Say it! Demand it to stop! Pull that word up from way down deep in your womb! Pull it up from that most heavenly place that holds your future, your future children, your future grandchildren. Say it! Say it girl! Say it! STOP! STOP! STOP! STOP!

Oh, my poor lil girl, I am so sorry to have to inform you that you have only just begun! My dearest girl, who is not so lil anymore, your journey to wholeness will be long and hard, but I think you can do it! You see, you are free from he but there has been a huge mistake, there is just a barnacle infested tiny shell left in his wake. A barnacle encrusted beautiful shell clinging to a skin tearing jagged rock. A rock so full of pride, strength, and power that you feel ashamed. No, you feel envy! Oh envy, your familiar friend. The green-eyed (you wish) monster that made you so passive-aggressively splash water in Maria's face because her braids were longer than yours, her clothes were nicer than yours, and all the boys loved her. Oops, so sorry you little bitc— . . . I mean, it was an accident. It was then that you began to realize that guys enjoyed a girl with longer hair than yours, lighter skin than yours, a bigger butt than yours, and more outspoken than you have ever been.

You cute lil mouse of a girl, just there being invisible and in your own little imaginary world. My lil girl, that cage is beginning to cave in! Your monster is seeping out!

I see you, my young lady. You have been blessed with a mom that appreciates education, family, and thankfully, therapy. Momma made sure you were able to come to terms with the horrible things you had to experience. I watched you really look forward to the chocolate milkshake during your time with the therapist, and the cheeseburger was the icing on the cake. You would draw, write, and talk forever for a dang cafeteria cheeseburger. I know that you still think about the things you don't or won't remember, but it's okay. I still love you. I love you unconditionally because you are a worthy, beautiful Black diamond in the rough! Keep fighting, my sweetheart, keep fighting.

Where are you, my lil girl? I suppose I should refer to you as my young lady or my beautiful lady, since you aren't a little girl anymore. You have come so far from that innocent lil girl that only wanted to be accepted, respected, and loved, but I see your monster has escaped. You are no longer my shy and quiet little butterfly. You are demanding of attention and controlling! Why does it hurt your soul if a man doesn't call? Does it mean you aren't worthy of his attention, his love? I know it is not for me to interfere, but I wish I could stop you from going down this hole. Please use the skills that you worked so hard to gain and look within yourself. Seek refuge in knowing that he doesn't matter, you do! My love, you are on the verge of becoming a stalker. You can't make him love you! You can't make him need you! Now the pain of rejection, the shame of losing control, and the confusion of not knowing why men won't love you like you want to be loved has set in. I fear for you and I really hope you can glean some inner confidence from your invisible companion within the mirror. I am so sorry you have to go through this process, my lil angel. It seems you take two steps forward and seven steps back, but don't worry, I still love you. We still love you.

You are a mom now! You have come so far from that innocent lil girl that used to seek asylum in the mirror. The woman in the mirror is getting impatient. She has only been privy to observing you grow into this most amazing woman from within the mirror. We are both anticipating the date, hour, and minute of your integration, but, until then, we are meant to wait. I am forced to wait in the corners of your beautiful mind as you tend to hide there. My lady, I need you to wake up. Wake up! You have been asleep for a very longtime. Your time is here! My time is here! The woman in the mirror's time is here!

The stresses of this world have worn you down, my queen, and I can't help you. This is a battle you must fight on your own. I believe in you, my heart. The days blend into each other as you perform your duties as a single mother. You aren't here; where are you? Where are you hiding? Your mind is a prison made up of denial, pain, and disappointment. I see why you hide. I see the fear of failure and exhaustion from doing it on your own. You have learned to tough it out and get it done by any means necessary. Your role models are all strong, intelligent, and successful women whom you are proud to join in the fight, but you want more. Secretly, you know there is more for you than this day-to-day banality. Reality sucks the hope out of you, and you retreat into the secret place again, into that cocoon of familiarity and safety. Why do you hide from us? Why do you hide from the world? When you shine, you are the sparkle in someone's eye. You are the sparkle in your children's eyes, but you know that so you remain present enough for them. The time has come for you to wake up! Wake up, my love! Wake up! Crawl out of that corner in your mind and be present. Not for me or anyone else, but for you. You must wake up for you! There is so much that needs to be done! I see you, my darling, and I am here to catch you if you fall. Get up now!

I see you, my sweetheart; I see you looking in the mirror, but this time you hesitate. What do you see? With joy I realize you see her! You see YOU! The you that I have been waiting for you to see. My beautiful queen, you are enough! You are worthy! You are loved unconditionally! You ARE love! The woman inside the mirror reaches for you and you slowly reach back. When your hands connect, it is like lightning in the sky with all the electric energy being shared with the world. You feel the energy, the love, the strength, and the power that has been imprisoned within your lack of self-esteem and limiting self-concept. Your hesitation is replaced with elation as you realize that it has been you inside the mirror all along! You step out of the mirror and into yourself. Your whole self!

Oh, my sweet girl, I am so proud of you! You are doing the difficult work of healing. You are seeking change and accepting what has been and what is. Positivity and an unbending belief in all things good have allowed you to be grateful for just being. You are grateful for surviving breast cancer. You are grateful for surviving childhood sexual abuse. You are grateful for surviving a lifelong battle with social anxiety and depression. The blessings abound when it comes to you. You made it, my sweet girl! You made it through it all! We have anticipated this union and have been so patient over the years. We have been waiting for you, knowing everyone comes to terms with their greatness in their own time.

I would like to say I have not fully come to terms with my greatness at this point in my life, but I have begun to get there. What I will say is I am aware of my greatness. My journey to wholeness and living life as my true self continues, and I am fine with that. I live each day being present! Regardless of the level of difficulty, I am present!

About the Visionary Author

Author Mia Turner-Whitley is a contributing author of three books, "No Glory Without A Story," "Phenomenal Woman: Still Standing" and Amazon Best Seller, "The Mom in Me"! "When I Was A Child" is her first anthology as a Visionary Author, and definitely not her last. Mia wants to provide a platform where people can share their life experiences and also teach individuals the business side of being an author. Mia believes that the traumatic, pain or failures in life that have turned to success need to be shared because our triumphs are not just for personal healing and growth, but to help someone else on their journey.

Mia is a true family person! She also loves encouraging and uplifting others. She has over 25 years of customer service and leadership training, and over 15 years of public service facilitating married, engaged and parenting classes. Mia is also Assistant Director of Pretty Blessed Girls mentoring program. MIASpeaks provides transformational speaking, coaching, training or writing, virtually or in person. She is originally from East St Louis/Washington Park, IL.

Mia currently resides in Dallas, TX with her husband, children, grandchildren, sister, nephew and lots of friends and family!

Made in the USA
Columbia, SC
27 December 2022

74990416R00070